A Nantucket Christmas

A Nantucket Christmas

LESLIE LINSLEY

PHOTOGRAPHY BY JEFFREY ALLEN

BULFINCH PRESS

NEW YORK BOSTON

Bulfinch Press

Time Warner Book Group

1271 Avenue of the Americas, New York, NY 10021

Visit our Web site at www.bulfinchpress.com

First Edition

Library of Congress Cataloging-in-Publication Data

Linsley, Leslie.

   A Nantucket Christmas / Leslie Linsley ; photographs by Jeffrey Allen.

     p. cm.

   ISBN 0-8212-2871-4

     1. Christmas—Massachusetts—Nantucket. 2. Christmas decorations—Massachusetts—Nantucket.

3. Nantucket (Mass.)—Social life and customs. I. Title.

   GT4896.M4L56 2004

   394.2663—dc22   2004045118

Design by Joel Avirom, Jason Snyder, and Meghan Day Healey

Printed in China

*To the people and organizations
who strive to preserve the
natural beauty and historic
treasures of Nantucket*

⇥⨯⇤

CONTENTS

Introduction:
A Nantucket Christmas
ix

1

A Christmas Stroll Around Nantucket
3

2

Christmas in Early Island Homes
23

3

Ready to Entertain
59

4

Personal Pleasures
119

5

Celebrating in Style
159

Acknowledgments
193

INTRODUCTION

A Nantucket Christmas ➤✕◀

NANTUCKET ISLAND is a little patch of earth located thirty miles off the coast of Cape Cod, Massachusetts. The island can be reached only by boat or by plane, and it is the isolation from the mainland that has been partially credited with keeping its natural beauty and charm intact.

Just seven miles wide and fourteen miles long, this little spit of land in the Atlantic Ocean has managed to achieve a level of sophistication that comes from adapting to whatever is new and elegant while retaining an atmosphere of casual simplicity and its own traditions.

The island was discovered in 1602 by an Englishman, Captain Bartholomew Gosnold. Thomas Mayhew later purchased it in 1641, and for the next two hundred years the island population grew and prospered into an established, self-contained community. In 1712 the first spermaceti whale was caught, launching an industry that helped to make Nantucket known throughout the world.

Over the years there were many setbacks: the discovery of petroleum put an end to the need for whale oil, and the Great Fire of 1846 destroyed a third of the town. As early as 1870, with the island's population at an all-time low and not a ship to its name, some inventive people began to promote Nantucket as a tourist attraction, a place to enjoy the sea air and healthy environment.

Nantucket has surpassed the wildest dreams of those first visionaries and is now a world-class summer resort. Today there are more than ten thousand year-round residents on the island, and the population swells to more than thirty-five thousand during the summer months. However, while it is known as a summer vacation place, it is the off-season that islanders love best.

In the winter months the island's community spirit is more evident than at any other time of year. Islanders know, or at least recognize, one another and no one is in any particular hurry, always taking time to chat with an acquaintance when getting mail from the post office in town, stopping at the Hub for the paper, or shopping in the local supermarket.

The winter brings out the characteristics of a beautiful New England town steeped in history. In this quiet season, Nantucket homes are beehives of creative activity. Entertaining is a big part of island life, and Christmastime on the island is particularly special. The community becomes extremely social during the holidays, when friends gather to catch up on each other's lives, share food, and gossip. Most homeowners take great pride in their houses and enjoy sharing them with others.

Nantucket has been named one of America's endangered places by the National Trust for Historic Preservation. The houses in town were all built in the 1800s and have been inhabited ever since. The annual Holiday House Tour, which showcases houses beautifully decorated for Christmas, gives visitors an opportunity to go into a select few of these private homes each year, some of which we have been fortunate to photograph for inclusion in this book. Many of the houses we photographed were chosen for their architectural and historic interest and their special decorations.

Nantucket has always stood for individuality and diversity in all things, and while many of the homes are antiques, there are other, newer homes that are decorated in more contemporary styles. These are represented here as well.

We have endeavored to show off our island at its prettiest, in December, when Nantucket looks like an old-fashioned Christmas card, as islanders take special care to decorate their homes with traditional bowers and garlands of evergreens, holly, winterberries, seashells, and pinecones. The shops in town are decorated as well, and Main, Centre, Federal, and India Streets are lined with Christmas trees that are ceremoniously lit at sundown on the Friday after Thanksgiving.

"Over the river and through the woods, to grandmother's house we go" is an old refrain that evokes images of Christmas long ago. Although we hardly travel by horse and buggy anymore, we still maintain many of the traditions associated with the past, especially those of small towns throughout the country. Perhaps this is why our island has become such a popular place to spend the holidays.

And so, during this particularly beautiful time of year, we invite you to participate in island living through our eyes, whether joining us at our annual Festival of Trees or on a Christmas Stroll weekend, eavesdropping on a holiday party, or vicariously experiencing the romance and nostalgic qualities of Christmas in a quaint, historic village—if only for a little while.

A Nantucket Christmas

1 *A Christmas*

Stroll Around Nantucket

The Christmas Stroll →×←

During the first week of December, the Nantucket Chamber of Commerce in conjunction with the Merchants' Association puts on a festival that has traditionally drawn visitors to the island from all around the globe. Stores are decorated and serve hot cider and home-baked cookies, and local groups decorate the outdoor trees with a theme. Main Street is cordoned off for pedestrians only, and there is much merriment with carolers, Santa's arrival, and many activities offered to one and all.

On Nantucket much of the mainland commercialism passes us by. There are no malls, no chain stores, not even overhead stoplights, which makes it easy to concentrate on the spirit of the holidays—creating gifts and decorating our homes, visiting with friends, and, in general, feeling a sense of community. Celebrating Christmas on Nantucket offers visitors a less harried alternative to today's often frenetic holiday season.

The Christmas Stroll is for anyone who would like to experience the joy of the season in a small town. There are craft shows, art exhibits, raffles, carolers and theatrical performances, guided historical walking tours, dancers, bell ringers, musicians, bazaars and puppet shows, food tents, and even a ghost walk. Many who come here find they are a bit nostalgic for what

OPPOSITE: *Santa is driven in a horse-drawn buggy to the historic Pacific National Bank building at the head of Main Street, where children eagerly await his arrival.*

ABOVE: *Town crier Curtis Barnes rings the bells on Main Street to welcome visitors and islanders to the Christmas Stroll festivities.*

they may have had as children—or wish they had had. It is also a way for many to give their children a sense of old-fashioned community celebration. My mother used to say that what we do with our children gives us the opportunity to create memories for the future.

A concerted effort is made to maintain a level of quality throughout the island, whether in the stores, restaurants, hotels, or services, which makes this place so special year-round, but most certainly during the holidays.

Around Town

❯❯❮❮ THE JARED COFFIN HOUSE

This popular inn in the center of town was originally built as a private residence by Jared Coffin, a prominent ship owner, in 1845. When it was refitted as a hotel in 1887 it was called the Ocean House. The basement was converted to a billiard saloon, and the Tap Room remains today as a restaurant and after-work gathering place favored by locals and vacationers alike.

In 1961 the property was purchased by the Nantucket Historic Trust and completely restored as the Jared Coffin House, a twenty-six-room year-round hotel. Phillip and Margaret Read purchased the inn in 1976. Today, the JC House (as it is commonly known) includes various other historic buildings, for a total of sixty rooms.

During the Christmas season (Thanksgiving to New Year's Day), the inn is decked out in all its holiday finery. The stone steps in front lead up to a massive door that is traditionally decorated with a handmade cranberry wreath commemorating Nantucket's harvest. The Christmas tree stands in the front parlor, and a fire is always blazing in the lovely old fireplace. The mantels are strewn with greens, and the gracious stairway banister is wound with garlands. The formal dining room is also decorated in the traditional style of the island.

LEFT: *The Jethro Coffin House on Sunset Hill was built in 1686 and is believed to be the oldest on the island. Today it is open to the public and, with its period furnishings, offers a peek into what life in the seventeenth century might have been like.*

OPPOSITE: *Built in 1845, the Jared Coffin House at 29 Broad Street is the oldest continuously operating inn on Nantucket. At Christmastime the inn provides a lovely traditional setting for guests who want a romantic Nantucket experience.*

⇥⊰ UNITED METHODIST CHURCH

The Nantucket United Methodist Church, erected in 1823, stands at the corner of Main and Centre Streets. Extensive improvements were made in 1840 when the pulpit, originally in the front of the church, was relocated to the rear, where it now stands, and the pews were turned to face it. A new gable roof was built on top of the old one, and an impressive portico with six Ionic pillars was added.

The simplicity and strength of the design reflect the sturdy character and reverence of the seafaring men who built the church. That quality is seen in the deep paneling of the balconies, the single wide board that forms the pew back, and the mahogany top rail that has no intricate carving but ends in a graceful swirl. The paneled door of each pew, so quaintly reminiscent of another era, originally served the practical purpose of holding in the heat of the foot warmers provided by each pew holder. The pew holders also installed custom-built hymnal racks and armrests in their pews. In 1995 a nonprofit organization composed of members of the church and community formed the Two Centre Street Restoration Project for the purpose of restoring the building.

ABOVE, TOP: *Strands of clear lights and starfish ornaments cover the live trees at the front of the United Methodist Church.*

ABOVE, BOTTOM: *To continue the simple theme, Donna Elle's design team hung an evergreen wreath decorated with a single starfish ornament in each of the massive floor-to-ceiling windows of the church.*

OPPOSITE: *United Methodist Church at Two Centre Street was built in 1822–23. The ceiling is supported by sixty-foot-long, twelve-by-twelve handhewn beams, which were brought to the island on whaling ships. The building is both a historic architectural gem and an active center for worship, community meetings, and the performing arts. In 1999 then First Lady Hillary Clinton visited this site and made the building part of the Save America's Treasures program, a joint effort of the National Trust for Historic Preservation and the White House. A rare Appleton pump organ, built in Boston in 1831, was installed in the 1850s; it is one of only five in existence. Donna Elle Interior Design executed the simple holiday decorations in keeping with the building's architectural style.*

OVERLEAF: *Brant Point Lighthouse is one of three lighthouses on the island and has been protecting Nantucket Harbor since 1746. It sits on an accessible beach a short walk from town. As the steamship rounds the point, the lighthouse is the first historic landmark visitors see before entering Nantucket Harbor. When leaving, the saying goes, "If you throw a penny overboard as you round Brant Point, you will surely return to the island."*

The Festival of Trees →×←

The Nantucket Historical Association is an important organization, responsible for the upkeep and operation of many historic sites on the island, including two museums and a research library. Their collection represents many definitive aspects of Nantucket's history, such as whaling, land and sea transportation, the Quaker religion, fine and decorative arts, farming, commerce, and architecture. The library contains more than forty-five thousand photographs and thousands of books and manuscripts, including an outstanding collection of whale-ship logs.

One of their most popular fund-raising events is the annual Festival of Trees held throughout the month of December. The Whaling Museum, featuring artifacts from Nantucket's days as a nineteenth-century whaling empire, including a full-size whale skeleton, is the site for this celebration. Fifty Christmas trees are brought in and local artists, designers, business owners, and community groups decorate each with a theme. A preview party is held on Thursday evening before Stroll weekend begins; members buy their tickets well in advance, as it is always a sold-out affair. Local restaurants donate their time and food, and it's a chance for islanders, visitors, and museum supporters to kick off the holiday season. The trees are then on exhibit for the entire month, and the museum is open to the public every weekend through Christmas.

OPPOSITE: *Inside the Nantucket Whaling Museum, the decorated trees add a festive air to this historic building. The Fresnel lens, used in the nineteenth century in the 'Sconset lighthouse, now hangs prominently in the museum.*

ABOVE: *Decorated trees covered with tiny, clear fairy lights create a magical walkway for visitors to view the trees. This part of the museum has recently been completely renovated and expanded.*

LEFT: *The main room of the Nantucket Whaling Museum houses a fully equipped whaleboat. Harpoons and other related nautical gear hang on the walls all around the room. Visitors get a double treat during the month of the Tree Festival, as Nantucket is proud to show off this authentic and extensive exhibit.*

SELECTING A TREE

The following are some tips for selecting a tree:

———✦———

Spruce trees have sharp needles. They are great for holding large, heavy ornaments.

———✦———

Balsam and Fraser firs are very fragrant and hold needles for a long time.

———✦———

Scotch and white pine cost the least and are the most popular. Although their branches are not strong enough to support heavy ornaments, they last a long time and smell good.

———✦———

Run your hand gently over a branch. If the needles feel dry and fall off easily, the tree isn't very fresh. Look for one that stays put under the hand test.

LIGHTING THE TREE

In keeping with the simple Nantucket style of decorating, most Nantucketers cover their trees with miniature clear lights. Lots of lights make a tree sparkle. To figure out the minimum number of lights needed, multiply the diameter of the tree (in feet) by eight, then multiply that number by the height of the tree (also in feet). If, for example, your tree is four feet in diameter and five feet tall, you would multiply four by eight, then thirty-two by five, for a total of 160 lights.

OPPOSITE: *Built in 1818, this imposing Federal-style brick structure with its raised granite foundation and curved front steps looms at the head of Main Street. In 1914 a music teacher in the Nantucket school system led a group of carolers around town, stopping to sing in front of the bank; and on Christmas Eve 1915, the first community Christmas tree on Nantucket was set up in front of the bank to celebrate the festive season. To this day, Nantucketers gather here for caroling at Christmastime. Now we have a Magical Talking Christmas Tree, which sits in front of the bank and entertains children waiting to see Santa. On a snowy day schoolchildren create their own interpretations of a winter bank customer.*

Deck the Doors →✕←

In the nineteenth century, when the Quakers dominated the island, there were hardly any changes during the month of December—no adornments of any sort on doorways, and certainly no wreaths. And even though newly settled Nantucketers indulge in lighted shrubbery here and there or string Christmas-tree lights along picket fences, door decorations remain rather simple.

→✕← FIRST IMPRESSIONS

A decorated front door is the very first impression you give to welcome guests during the holidays. Many Nantucketers hang a simple wreath or pine branches even before Thanksgiving weekend. Since the houses in town are close together and close to the street, passersby can enjoy these holiday touches. A festive mood is easy to create with anything from a few branches of greens tied with a bow to a wreath made of scallop or mussel shells. Perhaps the most celebrated house decoration in town is the cranberry wreath that hangs on the beautiful, massive door of the Jared Coffin House (see below).

MAKING A CRANBERRY WREATH

Fresh, hard cranberries, straight pins, and a straw or foam wreath-form are all that is needed to make a cranberry wreath. If the wreath is wrapped in plastic, there is no need to remove it. Simply secure the cranberries to the wreath-form with a long pin stuck through the center of each berry. Arrange the cranberries in very tightly packed circles to cover the entire front of the form. The back of the form may be left bare, as it will be placed against the front door. Hang with a loop of monofilament or fishing line.

OPPOSITE: *The pineapple design of the brass knocker on the front door of the Jared Coffin House inn symbolizes "welcome"; the handmade cranberry wreath is symbolic of Nantucket's cranberry harvest.*

ABOVE: *A simple red cranberry wreath hangs on the plain board door of this early island home.*

RIGHT: *The Christopher Starbuck House, one of the oldest houses on Nantucket, was first built in 1690 and later relocated from its original site in Sherburne, Nantucket's first settlement, to its present site on Main Street.*

✦✦ FESTIVAL OF WREATHS

Each year the Nantucket Historical Association sponsors a Festival of Wreaths featuring an array of creatively designed wreaths that are exhibited at Preservation Hall on Thanksgiving weekend. The main attraction of this special event is the silent auction for the wreaths, which have grown in number from fifty to over eighty different designs. The growing popularity of this event has attracted a wide range of designers, from artists to businesspeople, and from the Boys & Girls Club to senior groups. Each year, as more of the community gets involved, the wreaths get more varied. The Festival of Wreaths, a more casual event than the Festival of Trees, is also open to the public.

TOP, LEFT: *A lavish wreath, by Nantucket standards, is adorned with fruit and ribbons and hangs on the window of Mitchell's Book Corner at the top of Main Street. Wreaths on in-town buildings tend to be more elaborate than those found on houses.*

TOP, RIGHT: *"Nauma," an Indian name meaning "Sandy Point" (now Great Point), is the location of one of the three lighthouses on the island. Located in the village of Siasconset on the eastern end of the island, this little whale house, as they were called, was once a fishing shack. Those who crave a simple existence, if only for a few weeks a year, have turned these charming cottages into summer homes. Some are just as they were in the 1700s.*

BOTTOM, LEFT: *In keeping with the style of this house, built in 1740, a simple wreath of greens dotted with local berries adorns the front door.*

BOTTOM, RIGHT: *Typical Nantucket doors are paneled and have transom lights above. Other typical features include a simple stoop, railings with square balusters, and newel posts. Scallop shells, plentiful on Nantucket, are often used as wreath decoration.*

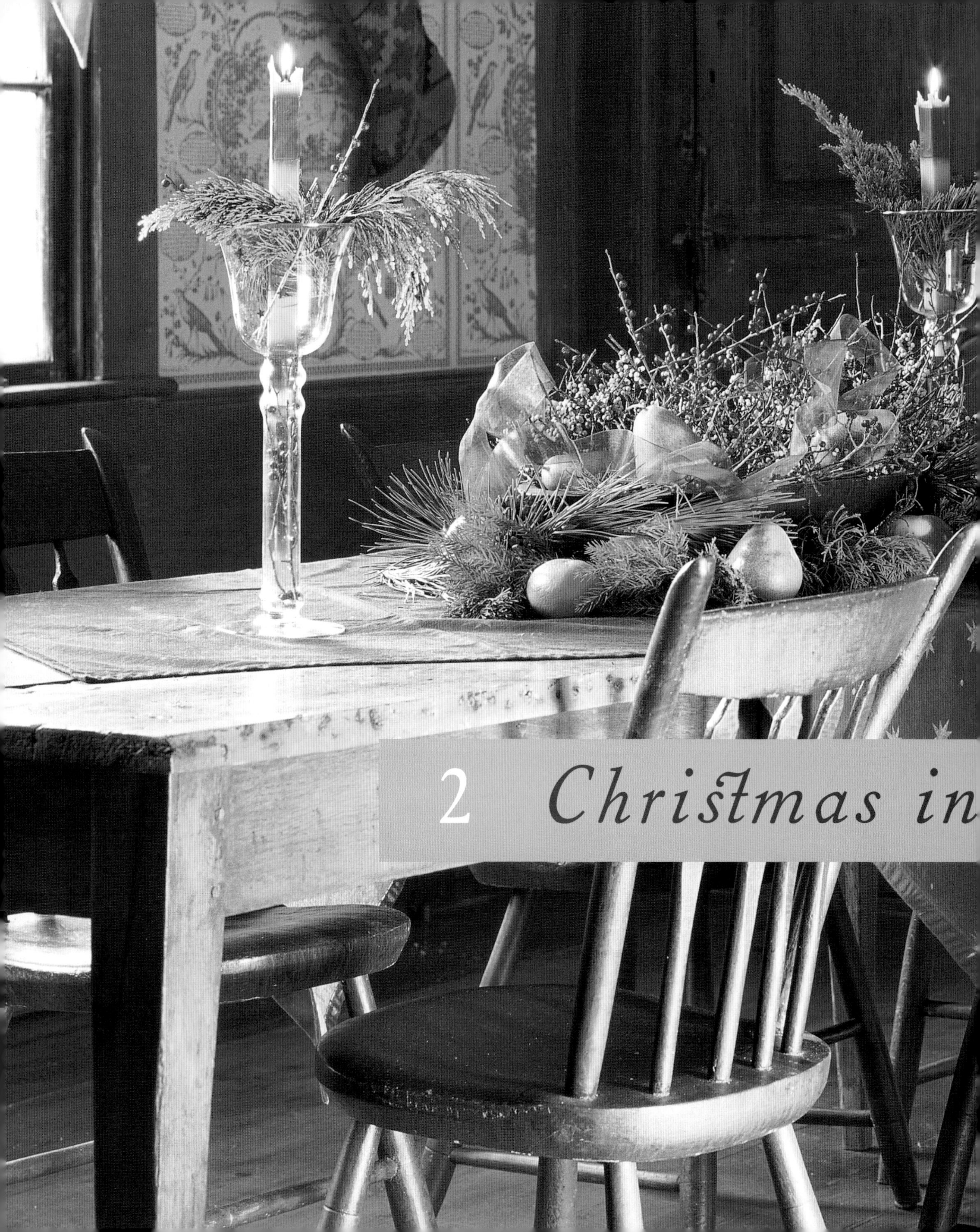

2 Christmas in

Early Island Homes

Small Wonder ➤✕◄

Mellie and Jim Cooper live in a gem of a house, built in 1830. Its small size is what attracted them to buy it fourteen years ago. "Our progressive parties usually start here," Mellie says. "The house is too small for sit-down dinners with more than two or three couples, but it's perfect for cocktails." The Coopers have restored the authentic beauty of this early home way beyond its humble beginnings. Mellie is an artist who works on hand-cast paper that she creates and paints to look like textured, three-dimensional items such as hooked rugs, christening dresses, and sailor's valentines. Represented by the Janis Aldrich Galleries (see page 186), she always sells

out her one-woman shows, and her work hangs in homes all over the country. The finished house is a result of this creative couple's collaborative effort. Together they had the vision to bring out the architectural beauty of the interior, with its worn, patinaed, wide pine floorboards, doorways with transom, and paneled walls, making it comfortable for today's

OPPOSITE: *The Christmas tree in the front hallway is covered with unusual chartreuse and celadon ornaments to complement the warm color of the wood on the stairway wall, the front door, and folk-art cabinet. The original wide pine floorboards are worn to a soft patina and reflect the lights on the tree and the scallop lights in the scallop basket. Greens and folk-art pieces are arranged on the wall and cabinet with miniature trees, tiny white flowering narcissus, and a string of scallop lights.*

ABOVE: *The little Quaker house, located on one of Nantucket's most historic in-town byways, has been meticulously restored beyond its humble beginning.*

OPPOSITE: *The antique table holds an unusual ivory box found in a local antiques shop and antique Royal Doulton vases that once belonged to Mellie's mother. One of Mellie's paintings of lace with tulip reflected in the mirror hangs beside a bamboo corner shelf unit holding white poinsettia plants in milk-glass vases, part of Mellie's collection.*

LEFT, TOP: *At one end of the living room a drop-leaf dining table provides workspace for Mellie to paint. Two simple wreaths on each window and a chair on either side of the table appeal to Mellie's sense of symmetry. The sleigh is intertwined with ivy and moss and filled with chartreuse balls. A teal candleholder brightens the tabletop.*

LEFT, BOTTOM: Christmas Purse *by Mellie Cooper (courtesy of the Janis Aldrich Gallery) hangs between the windows. The purse is made of hand-cast paper and meticulously painted with an old-fashioned winter scene.*

living without compromising its past. This year they removed a kitchen "wart" (a term used to describe an addition to the original house) that was literally falling off the house and replaced it with one that is up to date but still retains the exquisite integrity of the rest of the house.

In keeping with its simple Quaker origin, Mellie adds appropriate decorations at Christmastime. "I've always used real materials," she says, "but this year I found some really fabulous artificial greenery at Flowers On Chestnut (see page 161) and it actually looked better than the real thing. I had to smell it to believe it wasn't real." Wherever she has candles on the greens, such as on the mantel, she uses artificial greens, as doing so is safer in such an old house. Her classic approach to decorating extends to adding Christmas touches that accentuate her collections and furnishings rather than calling attention away from the overall look of the rooms. For example, she's taken the

OPPOSITE: *One of three small bedrooms upstairs, this one has the original working fireplace from the 1800s. The wallpaper is new but emulates the original. Greens on the mantel are dotted with votives in dessert-wine pressed glasses, and early pots hold delicate pink flowering plants, appropriately coordinated with the wallpaper. Touches of greens on the bed tray and a stark miniature tree on the desk fill the room with Christmas cheer. Botanical prints are from Janis Aldrich Gallery.*

LEFT: *Mellie Cooper painted the pale green and white stripes on the wall of the living room. The scalloped wooden window valances were custom made. The table is covered with sprigs of gold-sprinkled ivy, and a garland of magnolia leaves tops the mirror, purchased on-island.*

BELOW: *Celadon place mats, white milk-glass plates and glasses, and a handmade beaded sprig tied with an organdy ribbon at each place create an understated table setting for a holiday dinner. Clusters of beaded grapes encircle the unusual chandelier over the table.*

OPPOSITE: *Mellie's milk-glass collection has grown to include some wonderful pieces for setting the table with panache. Sugared grapes fill a lovely openwork bowl, a little chicken salt dish is one of a set, goblets, vases holding poinsettias, and a compote dish are used to make a lovely grouping on the table.*

Milk glass, named for its milky-white color, is a molded glass intended to look like porcelain, but it is much less expensive to produce. Older pieces can be traced back as far as the 1500s, but most of what is collected today is from the 1700s on. Milk glass was used to make all sorts of items—dishes and cups, boxes, vases, figurines, perfume bottles, match holders, and even lanterns. Some pieces are figural in design, incorporating flowers and animals such as cows and roosters. Christmas bulbs, parrots, Santas, trees, sleds, and other decorations were also made of milk glass. Milk glass is decorated in many different styles and techniques and lends itself to hobnail, a raised pattern of bumps, and lace, in which the glass simulates the look of lace. Hand-painted pieces are also common.

time to find celadon and chartreuse ornaments to complement the celadon color scheme used on the walls and fabrics throughout the house.

Mellie Cooper, a self-described "consummate treasure hunter," knows how to zero in on what's really worth owning. "I look for great stuff at great prices everywhere I go and combine flea-market finds with interesting, unusual antiques. The things I buy for the house don't necessarily have provenance, but they have to be stylish, with some wonderful detail that makes a piece interesting," she says.

"I love symmetry, and when I arrange the furniture I lean in that direction." Mellie is meticulous about details when creating little holiday vignettes on tabletops, along the fireplace mantels, and in the front hallway. Whether it's decorating for Christmas or for everyday living, she approaches it as she does her artwork, with confidence and decisiveness, and the results are seamless. There is something interesting everywhere you look.

The sitting room, behind the living room, is where the family relaxes by the fire. The mantel is covered with greens and little bunches of deep red berries. The stockings are hung in anticipation, one for each of the Coopers' children, Courtney, Jamie, and Delilah, featured in Mellie's painting over the mantel. Gold candles opposite the miniature paperwhites add the perfect finishing touch. A Minton chocolate service sits on the table by the fire.

A Christmas Wedding at Home →×←

There is nothing so romantic as a holiday wedding on Nantucket. The day of this wedding, the snow began to come down as if on cue, creating a magical environment for the guests, most of whom were arriving from Nashville. The front of the house is festooned with a garland of greens and fresh fruit; inside, the mantels are draped with pine branches and lots of tiny glass votive candles. Every room was brimming with flowers elegantly arranged by Flowers On Chestnut (see page 161). Children, dogs, extended family, and friends congregate in the sun-filled kitchen for a pre-wedding lunch. There is activity all around, and the snow falling in heavy flakes outside heightens the celebratory air of excitement and anticipation.

Whale-ship captain Job Coleman built this Federal-style house on Main Street in the early 1830s. The cobblestones that line Main Street were brought back as ballast to weigh down the ships and then used to pave the main roads. While many visitors to the island complain about bumpy Main Street, Nantucketers are vehement about keeping it just the way it was originally created.

OPPOSITE: *The French wallpaper in the dining room was meticulously reproduced using original methods to achieve the texture, scale, and brushstrokes of wallpaper found in an early New England Federal-style house. All the silverware and serving pieces on the sideboard are family heirlooms.*

LEFT: *The new kitchen at the back of the house is the family hub. The topiary bear is a wedding gift from the new bridegroom's stepdaughter, who affectionately calls him "the bear." Decked out in holiday berries and fruit, the topiary will preside over the breakfast buffet when the family gathers for the wedding weekend.*

PAPERWHITE NARCISSUS

Paperwhite narcissus has a wonderful, strong fragrance and is easy to grow for the holidays. It's a lovely flower to bring freshness to any room at Christmastime. It blooms quickly and doesn't need soil. Simply find a pretty container approximately three inches deep and fill it halfway with pebbles, shells, or gravel. Set the bulbs on top and add water to cover them halfway. Keep watered and in about two weeks you will see blossoms; these bulbs will continue blooming for about four weeks.

OPPOSITE: *Typically, Federal-style houses have two rooms identical in size, one behind the other, on either side of the center hallway. To the left, opposite the front living room, is the front parlor. The chocolate-brown walls, glossy white Federal molding, deep mocha-colored sofa, and original pine floors are reminiscent of an earlier age and create a peaceful oasis in the heart of town. The mantel decorations mimic those in the living room, with pinecones and sticks of cinnamon on evergreens. A small bouquet of pink lilies and greens is set on a side table.*

ABOVE: *The center hallway leads straight back to the kitchen, where the family loves to gather to share an informal meal. The original wide pine floorboards date back to the 1800s. James Herbst gave the walls a faux-stone decorative paint treatment, much as one would find in fashionable early nineteenth-century interiors. The sideboard holds simple paperwhites in a silver bowl, and a continuous strand of greens winds around the banister, extending the holiday decorations to the upstairs rooms.*

The less-formal sitting room adjoins
the living room with sliding pocket doors
originally used to conserve heat. Small
bouquets of fresh flowers are tastefully
placed around the room among groupings
of family photographs and collectibles.
Pinecones, cinnamon sticks, and votive
candles are interspersed on fresh greens
that spill over the mantelpiece. Matching
topiaries in urns flank the sea serpent,
a wonderful piece of folk art.

The formal five-bayed, clapboard facade of this gracious Main Street home includes a center door surround with transom and double stairs, called a friendship stairway (one can approach the door from either side) after the Society of Friends and the tradition of welcoming others into their homes. Four end chimneys serve eight interior fireplaces in the sixteen-room house. The third-floor space once housed sailors from Captain Coleman's ship. The furnishings throughout are family treasures—many were wedding gifts handed down from bride to bride in the family. There is Grandmother's table and Great-Grandmother's silver, and a bridal clock from the 1800s that came from a grandmother in Charleston. Everything has a history here.

Today four generations enjoy both the house and the formal courtyard-style garden, with its traditional Nantucket plantings: boxwoods, roses, hydrangeas, wisterias, and an old euonymus hedge. "We really use and enjoy the house and feel we are part of its history," says the owner. "A house is never finished until the last family leaves it. I hope when I leave here my spirit is left in the house."

OPPOSITE, TOP: *Simple greens appropriately add holiday touches to the Federal-style house on Main Street. Fresh-fallen snow creates a magical setting for the wedding that is about to take place here.*

OPPOSITE, BOTTOM: *Candelabras, fresh greens, and an exquisite array of roses, tulips, lilies, and sprigs of holly adorn the marble mantelpiece of one of the six fireplaces in the house.*

ABOVE: *The holiday wedding greens and a lavish bouquet on the mantel decorate the elegant front room. Nothing detracts from the furnishings, most of which consist of family heirlooms. The rocking horse, a piece of early American folk art, lends an air of playfulness to the formal room.*

A Quaker Setting →×←

Built in 1811, the house at One Milk Street typifies the island's growing Quaker population of the time. The pilasters on the exterior doorway were thought to have been added during the Greek Revival movement of the mid-1800s.

Characteristically, a massive center chimney originally provided heating and cooking sources through numerous open fireplaces. Unlike the lean-to style, these houses have a more centralized, open floor plan for ease of movement throughout the home. A gracious stairway is found to the left side of the house rather than in the usual center location. An early beehive oven remains in the basement. The current owner, Luraye Tate, maintains this house in its original state and has made it homey and comfortable even in the high-tech age of the twenty-first century.

OPPOSITE: *The fireplace in this 1800s house was once used as a heat source and fills one wall in the living room. The simplest Christmas decorations can often be the most effective. Unembellished greens and sprigs of holly fill the mantel. Nautical collectibles such as this early ship model are typical accessories in Nantucket homes. Modern accents such as the red-and-white pillows create a holiday feeling along with the massive lightship basket filled with poinsettias on the hearth.*

ABOVE: *One Milk Street is typical of a Nantucket house built from the 1760s to 1830s. The house rises two and a half stories on a brick foundation with basement and is shingled on the exterior like others of its type. A simple evergreen wreath adorns the door, and clay pots on the porch are filled with pine branches and holly.*

During the island's Christmas Stroll weekend, a group of in-town houses is chosen and decorated by island interior designers for the Annual Holiday House Tour. This open-house tour is a rare opportunity for island visitors to see inside these privately owned residences. There is always a nice combination of small and grand homes as well as different architectural styles. This house, just off upper Main Street, represents one of Nantucket's earliest homes.

Holly McGowen of Coastal Design approached this project with great sensitivity and took care not to do anything that might upstage the original details of the house. When decorations began to creep into the Quaker existence, they came in the form of simple greens. A sprig of holly or a pine branch might have been pinned to a front door, and, until quite recently, a plain wreath made of greens was the decoration of choice.

LEFT: *Miniature apples fill the mantel over the fireplace in this breakfast room off the kitchen, and a child's bear is dressed up with a taffeta bow for the holidays. Sugar-cookies-in-the-making will soon be set out with eggnog in anticipation of Santa's arrival.*

OPPOSITE: *This early home is simply decorated in a country style. The red holiday accents, dark wood of the furniture, and original wide pine floorboards create a warm and inviting environment. Glass transoms over the doorways enabled the early settlers to know if there was a fire in a room, as doors were kept closed to conserve heat. The pine table is covered with a red cloth, and the centerpiece is a wooden bowl filled with berry branches gathered from the yard. The banister in the front hallway is wrapped with a fresh pine garland twined with white organdy ribbon. The red-and-white pillows and patchwork quilt, combined with pots of red and white poinsettias, add just the right country touch for the holidays. The antique bench is perfect for holding a few last-minute gifts.*

It would seem entirely in poor taste and totally out of character to use anything more elaborate than fresh boughs, twigs and berries (perhaps cut right from the yard), and fruit as adornments for these simple rooms. Holly brought in lots of fresh greens from the 'Sconset Gardener (owned by her husband) and decorated in a simple manner befitting the Quaker style of each room. She added cranberry and bayberry candles that might have been made by the original homeowners. The pine wreaths, with a simple white bow, adorning the front windows might not echo the Quaker sensibility, but they are appropriately modest by today's standards for celebrating the season and welcoming the island visitors in the spirit of Nantucket.

An early sideboard at one end of the dining room repeats the decorative theme of the table. A tin filled with red poinsettias offsets the grouping of candleholders made from old thread spools. The Quakers often hung extra chairs from peg rails mounted on the wall, as seen here.

Granted Wishes →×←

The Captain Charles Grant house on Orange
Street was built in 1832 using only copper nails.
Its original owner spent fifty-six years as captain
of a whaling ship. When Ernie and Kay Frank
bought the house in 1979, it seemed only fitting to
name the house Granted Wishes after its original
owner and to express their own feelings of good
fortune for the opportunity to live in it. The
Franks have traveled extensively all over the
world, and the house is filled with treasures they
have brought back with them. All the unusual
collectibles are displayed and used in much the
same way that Captain Grant and his family lived
in this house.

   While the house is grand and stately, sitting on its high foundation above street level,
the high-ceilinged rooms are not overly large. Fireplaces in each of the first-floor rooms add
to its comfortable ambience. Ernie and Kay and their three children love the house in all
seasons but admit that it is particularly special at Christmastime, when they all get together.
Kay loves decorating a tree for the front hallway with a special theme each year.

   The tree can only be described as regal. Decked in gold, silver, and red ornaments
and nestled into the corner under the curving staircase, it is the first thing one sees when

ABOVE: *This Greek Revival house on Orange Street is raised well above street level.
The wrought-iron banisters are decked with bayberry garlands; fresh greens encircle
the Ionic columns, and urns are filled with miniature pine trees and holly. A kissing
ball hangs under the portico.*

OPPOSITE: *Gifts wrapped in red shiny paper with lavish gold lamé ribbon surround
the ten-foot-high Christmas tree and spill out onto the floor. A grouping of white
poinsettia plants at the base of the staircase adds to the opulence of the entryway.*

entering the house. When the massive front door is left open, visitors get a glimpse of this spectacular sight. For just a moment one might even imagine a scene like this so long ago when Captain Grant and his family celebrated the holidays in this house. Traditions continue on Nantucket, and each family who occupies an early home becomes part of its history.

Even though their children are grown, Christmas-morning rituals haven't changed. The presents have simply turned into grown-up toys. Christmas Eve dinner is a formal affair, and Kay sets the table with all her favorite family treasures. "It can't be overdone," she says as she places the lace-edged napkins at each place setting.

ABOVE: *The apple painting over the marble mantelpiece sets the theme for the living room. A bowl of polished red apples sits on a Polynesian vessel that was once used as a storage barrel on board a ship.*

OPPOSITE: *The chest in the dining room came from a sailing vessel. An early crazy quilt made from velvet scraps creates a wonderful wall hanging, adding rich warm colors to one end of the room.*

CARE OF LINENS

Family heirlooms such as silverware and goblets and old-fashioned linen tablecloths with crocheted edgings that never get used any other time of the year make a table lovely during the holidays. To freshen linens that have been stored away for months, wash them and then let them air-dry until slightly damp. Press the linens on the wrong side while damp.

If a guest spills coffee on your best linen tablecloth, quickly rinse with boiling water before washing. Rub salt into fruit stains, then soak in cold water and wash in cold water as well.

To store linens away until next year, always wrap them in blue tissue or acid-free paper for protection from light damage. White tissue lets light in, which causes yellowing. Store in a dry place with good air circulation. Unbleached muslin is also a good material for wrapping linens.

A Traditional Setting

Orange Street is one of the main roads leading out of town from the top of Main Street, giving it a slight rise above sea level. This is where many captains of whaling ships built their homes in the 1800s. Roof walks were built atop the houses, and from here one can see far out into the harbor. Once called widow's walks, these rooftop decks provided a lookout from which the captains' wives could search the harbor for ships bringing their husbands home from long whaling journeys.

Judy Lee and her husband, Robert Schwarzenbach, live in one of these houses, built in 1832 at the peak of the whaling era. The couple especially enjoys living in a home with a history. As part of the year-round community, Judy is president of the Maria Mitchell Association, an organization of science, education, and research named for Nantucket's renowned scientist, who discovered a comet. The association provides classes for adults and children in all aspects of natural science. Robert is on the board of Nantucket Community Sailing, which offers sailing classes for all ages. He is also a sponsor of the Opera Cup Sail, an annual race of wooden boats in Nantucket Sound.

OPPOSITE: *Reproductions of wallpaper designed during the China-trade era fit perfectly in old houses, as seen in this hallway. The Federal molding with bull's-eye trim, wide pine floorboards, and leaded-glass windows are original to the house. A country pitcher holds sprigs of holly picked from the yard, and a Shaker basket holds ribbon-star ornaments on the rosewood serpentine writing desk. A little kissing ball hangs from the doorway.*

ABOVE: *This Greek Revival house, built in the 1800s, has a generous entryway with leaded-glass sidelights and a version of Doric columns. The guilloche (an ornamental border formed of two or more interlaced bands around a series of circles) is part of the original building. Judy Lee made the wreath for her front door from island materials: greens, berries, pinecones, and scallop shells.*

LEFT: *A tin ornament hangs from picture wire in the center of the wreath; the bow is made from a strip of burlap.*

BELOW: *In the Nantucket tradition, in-town houses are close together and sit right up to the brick sidewalk. At Christmastime everyone passing by enjoys the decorated houses all in a row.*

OPPOSITE: *Even the ledge over the radiator is decorated with greens and candles reflected in the hallway mirror. A wreath hanging in the hallway window was made from sugared fruit. Pine sachets made from old French dishtowel fabric add to the fresh pine scent. The newel post is topped with an ivory mortgage button, a Nantucket tradition from bygone years that symbolized the final mortgage payment.*

MAKING A FAN PLAQUE

1

To make two fan plaques you'll need a circular piece of pine thirty-six inches in diameter, cut in half. You'll need approximately twenty-two large magnolia or galax leaves all the same size for each plaque. If magnolia leaves are not available, substitute rhododendron or similar leaves. Secure three rows of nails, angled up and evenly spaced over the entire board, to hold the fruit.

2

Cut the stem ends off the leaves. Using a staple gun, attach most of the leaves to the top curve of the board in a fan shape so that they overlap each other and protrude outward 3 or 4 inches from the edge of the board.

3

Staple the rest of the leaves in a fan pattern over the entire board so that it is completely covered. If any of the board shows around the edges, staple leaves or sprigs of boxwood to cover it.

4

Try different placements of the fruit before actually attaching it to the board to be sure you have a pleasing arrangement. Impale a medium-size piece of fruit on each of the nails. Judy uses pomegranate, red Delicious apples, tangerines, pears, peppers, pinecones, and garlic on her plaques. The size and shape of the fruit determine its placement.

5

Equally space two screw eyes twelve inches apart at the top of the plaque and insert for hanging. Hang under a window (opposite).

After living in their house for several years, they built a one-story kitchen addition. Judy and Robert are avid cooks, and the kitchen was designed with two of everything so they could cook together. The modern kitchen melds the past with the present for comfortable living, and this is where everyone congregates.

These old houses are lovely to decorate for the holidays. One has only to add simple touches of flowers and greenery without detracting from the intrinsic beauty of the interior details. Judy especially likes to make her own decorations, and now that they have the new kitchen, there is a table big enough to accommodate all the evergreens and fruit and other materials to make her fan plaques. She attaches one under each of the front windows of the house. This year the couple is throwing a "drop-in" party, and Judy is making wreaths for the windows in the parlor. The finishing touches include a kissing ball hanging over the stairway in the front entryway and a sprig of mistletoe over the doorway. "You can't have a holiday party without it," Judy says.

3 Ready to Entertain

Rooted in History ✦

The early, in-town historic houses on Nantucket are
treasured as a link to the island's past. They tell a story
about the people who lived here and, as time goes on,
become more valued and valuable as a natural resource. In
1992, Ian and Carolyn MacKenzie bought one of these gems, a classic Nantucket house built in
1786 by whaler and merchant George Lawrence. The MacKenzies understand their part in the
continuation of the island's history and are dedicated to the island and preserving their home
with integrity for future generations. With sensitivity and understanding, they restored,
refurbished, and furnished their house, bringing out its full potential as a gracious yet modest
home, appropriate for living in the twenty-first century.

Carolyn says, "One of the things we like about having an antique house is the
quirkiness that comes from the use of old pieces of wood. Nothing was wasted. Some of

OPPOSITE: *Guests are met with holiday cheer as soon as they open the front door. A grouping of miniature
evergreens around a twig tree encircled with a garland of cranberries on a camphor chest is set up under
the front hall stairway. A garland of green and brown magnolia leaves festoon the banister. Completing
the traditional evergreen and cranberry color scheme are two Santas amid wrapped packages.*

ABOVE: *Miniature trees adorn an antique chest along with tasteful cranberry accents throughout the
entryway. The carved wooden swan adds graceful punctuation, as does the pure-white plate collection
on the wall. Holiday decorations necessitate no change of decor, just an extension of it.*

our supporting beams look like chewed-up ships' masts. Our living room wainscoting is made of recycled shutters. Hinge marks are still very evident."

This is a wonderful house for family gatherings and parties with friends. It is both intimate and expansive, with cozy rooms for curling up on cold evenings and the new addition of a "garden room" fit for the pre-wedding party the MacKenzies are hosting for Dorothy Slover and Doug Kenwood (see page 87). "Our new summer living room seems to be working as a winter gathering place as well," Carolyn notes.

The house is furnished with all sorts of interesting pieces found on trips abroad as well as with treasures uncovered from antiques shops and auctions on Nantucket. The couple has a passion for marine antiques and island collectibles, and Ian's important collection of scrimshaw, displayed in all the rooms, complements the historic period in which the house was built. Together these items represent pieces of another era and are a tribute to those who were dedicated to the sea.

This Christmas the buzz is all about the impending wedding, which makes the holiday all the more special for off- and on-island friends alike. The house is alive with the comings and goings of the bride-to-be, the future groom, the caterer, the florists, and a bevy

LEFT: *The Santa figure, appropriately holding a miniature tree in the crook of his arm, sits on top of an exquisite example of an early inlaid box.*

OPPOSITE: *The front sitting room is carefully furnished with well-placed marine art and collectibles, such as an early lightship basket and ivory flag on the drop-leaf coffee table. "I love drop-leaf tables because they're so versatile," Carolyn says. A few greens, a red bow, miniature trees, and a Santa perched on an inlaid box create a holiday mood without compromising the integrity of the room.*

OPPOSITE: *Greens and cranberries adorn an antique wood sideboard found on a trip to Ireland. Indicative of Carolyn's style is her attention to detail, like the candle wreaths, also found around the decanters, and use of cranberry candles surrounded by fresh Nantucket cranberries throughout.*

RIGHT: *A carved and painted wooden trunk from Portugal is perfect for holding a seasonal scene at one end of the new room.*

of friends and neighbors. Robin Bergland, flower designer and owner of Trillium, a shop in town, and her helper arrive with the flower arrangements. Kendra Lockley and her assistant arrive with the food (see her house on page 172) and immediately take over the kitchen. Mellie Cooper (see her house on page 25) pops in to make last-minute adjustments to the decorations that she and Carolyn arranged earlier.

The rooms are comfortably furnished and the holiday decorations are added sparingly, the classic evergreen and cranberry colors perfectly suited to the period and furnishings of the house. A few greens, unadorned trees and wreaths, cranberries, and candles everywhere are all it takes to infuse the rooms with the air of Christmas. Everything in this house is of a piece—timeless, classic, yet modern, creating a charming and welcoming invitation to join in the festivities.

Last year the owners added a large
family room with a dining alcove.
The high ceiling, lots of windows,
and a wall of French doors allow
light to flood the room, making this
a wonderful place for the family to
spend time together. Ian's scrimshaw
and Mellie Cooper's painting of a
sailor's valentine beside a bas-relief
sailboat fill the mantelpiece. The
room, carefully decorated with an
eclectic mix of furnishings from all
over the world, is proof that the past
and the present can be integrated
quite seamlessly. The ship's figure-
head is named Rose, after the ship
that bore her name.

67
→►◄◄
Ready to
Entertain

ABOVE: *Carolyn's collection of nutcrackers, brought out each year at Christmastime, fills the entire coffee table. Pinecones and greens, small poinsettias, Santas, a fisherman, two traditional Swedish painted wooden horses, and a tiny dwarf figure add to the playful nature of the scene.*

RIGHT: *The living room mantel holds an impressive collection of marine artifacts, including a sailor's valentine that reads "For My Sister," a pair of rare carved and colored walrus tusks depicting a slave owner and his slave, a ditty box, a whalebone barrel in the center, and a Mellie Cooper sailor's valentine painting on hand-cast paper. The carved-bone half hull of a sailing ship dominates the setting. Two whalebone busks are mounted below the mantel. One bears a small plaque in the center with the initials CM—the same as Carolyn's— inscribed on it, which gave Ian all the more reason to acquire it. Robin added appropriate holiday touches of bayberry leaves, pink baby pomegranates, and sprigs of winterberries. Three velvet stockings await the MacKenzie daughters.*

LEFT, TOP: *Later in the evening the harvest table will be set for the party. Intimate groups of six or seven will be spread out in the dining room, garden room, den, and here, off the kitchen. Robin has just delivered the floral arrangements with tall tapering candles, similar on each table. The bar is set for the party and decked out, and even the wall sconces have branches of fresh greens and ribbons attached.*

LEFT, BOTTOM: *An antique lantern illuminates carolers, a gift from Julie Parker, Carolyn's cousin who lives on Nantucket. "She's my only relative of the thirteen cousins I grew up with in Utah who lives in the East," she says. "Each Christmas Julie gave me a caroler until the collection was complete." Filling out the scene is a scrimshawed busk, a scrimshaw tooth on a stand, lady apples in a lightship basket, a folk-art mermaid, and a basket of holly.*

OPPOSITE: *A magical evening is about to happen. Kendra and her staff have covered the kitchen island with green velvet and lots of fresh greens, large crimson pomegranates, apples, ripe red plums, pears, and persimmons, with cranberries liberally sprinkled around the platters for the buffet dinner. The breadsticks fresh out of the oven fill a glass beaker. Votives dotting the greens add sparkle to the table. When it's partytime, every candle in the house is lit.*

PAGE 72: *The mosaic table, usually outside on the patio, has been pulled into service inside for the evening. Robin has placed one of the floral arrangements in the center. Plain evergreen wreaths hang in each window, and a garland of greens and berries is tastefully draped across the ceiling beam of the dining area. How could the guests not feel properly feted?*

PAGE 73: *The wine is poured and the first course is served. Fresh Nantucket bay scallops are a celebrated island delicacy worldwide, best enjoyed at the height of scallop season. Most islanders like their scallops lightly sautéed with a few fresh herbs, just the way Kendra makes them. Goat cheese and cranberry chutney is served in tortilla cups.*

MAKING A FLORAL CENTERPIECE

Robin Bergland, owner of Trillium, on Centre Street, approaches every project, from a simple floral bouquet to an outdoor wreath for a Main Street house, with originality and elegance. "I like extremes," she says. "It might be a minimal look or completely over the top. It depends on the home, the owner's taste, and the occasion." Robin's style is to work with the color scheme of the house and, whenever possible, to incorporate it into the arrangements.

She became interested in flowers as a little girl, when her grandmother introduced her to the beauty of nature. "I spent all my vacations with my grandparents in Baltimore growing up, and I always worked in the garden with my grandmother." Her first job at eighteen was in a flower shop in New York City and later as its manager. Robin has owned Trillium on Nantucket for five years and in that time has exquisitely created everything from the floral decorations for an extravagant wedding to a simple thank-you bouquet.

Flower-Arranging Tip

When placing roses into any arrangement, do it gently. First separate the areas around where you want to insert the rose stem, then poke it through. If the roses are manhandled, they will bruise in a few hours.

For the MacKenzie party she was careful not to upstage, but rather complement, the furnishings and buffet spread that Kendra was preparing for the pre-wedding party (see page 72). Carolyn and she decided there would be simple, elegant arrangements on each of the four dining tables, with each one contained in gold pedestals holding one tall taper.

Trillium, a flower shop on Centre Street, is a creative wonderland at any time of year, but during the holidays it is brimming with beautiful ornaments and all the fixings for decorating Nantucket houses. Unusual tabletop accessories can be found here along with fresh flowers brought in daily.

LEFT, TOP: *Robin Bergland created the floral centerpieces for the MacKenzie party (see page 72) and shows how they are made. She starts by lining the gold-leaf holder with wet moss around the outer edges. A plastic liner to fit the container is placed in the middle and filled with oasis.*

LEFT, BOTTOM: *Robin suggests starting with the largest flowers and adding the smallest last so they don't get buried in the arrangement. She begins by inserting a full hydrangea blossom into the middle of the oasis. Then she removes any bruised petals from the white roses and inserts them around the hydrangea. Robin does this in groups of six roses, all at the same height. It is important that the flowers are in full bloom and fat.*

RIGHT: *Robin fills in with greens and berries. (For this arrangement she used galax leaves.) She groups them in threes like a floret and cuts all stems together so they are the same length, then adds bay leaves, star eucalyptus, and protea, turning and inserting where needed until it is full. Bush ivy is stripped so that only the berries and a few leaves remain. Last, graceful tendrils of jasmine are inserted into the top. Tip: To avoid building a collar of one thing, be sure to alternate and zigzag greens so everything is at different heights.*

In the Grand Tradition ✦

Just up from the Pacific National Bank on Main Street sits a group of imposing houses built in the late 1700s to the early 1800s. These Federal-style houses, once owned by ship captains and heads of industry, represent a period of the greatest affluence in Nantucket's history and the dominant style of building in the 1830s. There are almost two hundred of these houses on Nantucket today, and Roy and Kathy Clauss and their five children live in one of them during the summer months and also celebrate the holidays there. Several alterations and additions have been made to the house but always in keeping with its original style.

This Federal-style house, built in 1828 for Matthew Crosby, is a two-and-a-half-story clapboard with a high brick basement, four end chimneys, a five-bayed asymmetrical facade, and a double stairway to the front door. The house is so soundly built that when one is sitting in the front living room, the rumble of cars going over the cobblestones past the house is hardly audible. During the day sunlight pours in from the oversize windows, accentuating the beauty of the rooms with their high ceilings and architectural grandeur. There are built-ins everywhere, and touches of whimsy along with elegance gives the house

OPPOSITE: *Pink and green are the dominating colors in the front living room, facing out onto cobbled Main Street. Donna Elle Interior Designs used this color scheme to decorate the eight-foot Christmas tree for the Twentieth Annual Holiday House Tour to benefit the children of Nantucket public schools. Even the piano is decked out with boughs of pine and oversize pinecones.*

ABOVE: *The front sitting room is decked out with nautical accessories, many of which have a star theme; the tree is covered with starfish to echo the theme. The lighthouse is a replica of Sankaty Head in the quaint fishing village of Siasconset on the eastern part of the island. Needlepoint stockings hang by the fireplace, and buckets of scallop shells sit on the hearth. Family photos fill shelves and tabletops.*

LEFT: *The casual breakfast room is done in a Swedish country style with an aqua and ivory theme. Painted kitchen chairs with country plaid cushions surround a scrubbed-pine table. Miniature pine trees line the window ledge, and each sill is decked with greenery and seashells gathered on many summer beachcombing afternoons.*

ABOVE: *Gingerbread men, fabric-wrapped balls topped with scallop shells, more shells holding candles, and red and green M&M's are all scattered across the table for a casual holiday breakfast decoration.*

a lived-in feeling. This family home is at once formal and comfortable and always bubbling with activity as friends and family come and go.

The layout of the house has a typical grand front entrance with the living room to the right and a sitting room or parlor opposite. There is a large family room in back of the living room and the formal dining room between the parlor and kitchen. A fireplace adorns every room, and during the winter, as the snow falls and the church bells chime the hours, everyone is nicely snuggled up beside a roaring fire. There's a Christmas tree decorated to match the pink living room, another in the parlor, and smaller trees in the kitchen and breakfast rooms. A pot of hot cider simmers on the kitchen stove, filling the room with warmth and good smells.

OPPOSITE: *A recent mural around the walls of the formal dining room recalls the style of nineteenth-century itinerant muralist Rufus Porter, known for his landscapes in the style of the Hudson River School. The mahogany table is set with family heirlooms. Silver and gold and everything that sparkles make this holiday setting special. Simple greens festooned with garlands of island cranberries, tall white candles in silver candlesticks, and a stone urn filled with a twig ball on a bed of greens decorate the center of the table. The sideboard holds silver bowls of pinecones and glass balls.*

RIGHT: *Each colorful linen napkin is tied with a satin ribbon and placed on a dinner plate. Sprigs of cinnamon, bay leaves, and winterberries are tucked under each ribbon. Gold-rimmed plates, glasses, and champagne goblets create festive place settings appropriately elegant in this room.*

A Whaling Bistro ➤⤙

The Brotherhood of Thieves, familiarly shortened by locals to "The Brotherhood," is a restaurant in a building built in 1847 and once a whalers' hangout. In the summertime, patrons wait in long lines to get into this popular, casual dining room with its denlike atmosphere, long tables, and boardinghouse-style service. In the winter months, this is a local haunt, where a fire is always blazing and the atmosphere convivial.

OPPOSITE: *The Brotherhood of Thieves, on Broad Street, was a whaling bar in the 1800s. Today it is a popular haunt for locals all year round. At Christmastime the entire staff decorates a tree and hangs stockings for one another all around the room.*

ABOVE: *Aside from casual burgers and fries, there is always an offering of daily dinner specials that includes local fare. The blackboards announce the changes of menu and specials each day. 'Tis the season for Nantucket bay scallops, and no self-respecting purveyor of food would be without this delicacy on its menu.*

Gracious Living ✦

Dorothy Slover bought and renovated the Francis Macy house in 1986, updating its infrastructure while maintaining its historic integrity. The house is a stunning example of gracious living on Nantucket, where the past is always part of everyday modern living. Each year, on the Saturday of Christmas Stroll weekend, Dorothy throws a champagne party and does it with panache. It is her style to casually invite friends and acquaintances as she meets them on the street, in the market, or while doing errands, never by formal invitation. The house itself provides all the formality one needs, and it is in this setting that one feels the grandeur of a house that was part of Nantucket's past as well as the comfortable atmosphere and spirit of the holidays created by its owner.

"I love a bit of decadence at this time of year, " Dorothy confides. She creates this with an abundance of fresh red tulips strewn over greens laid across the marble mantelpieces in the front parlor, living room, dining room, and library. It has become her signature

OPPOSITE: *The graceful sweeping central stairway is lined with pots of red poinsettias all the way up to the second floor. The boldly painted checkerboard floor is one of Dorothy's creations, a dramatic beginning for what's to follow.*

ABOVE: *This Main Street house, built in the 1800s, has a classically symmetrical facade. An Ionic portico creates a most dignified entranceway, raised templelike on a high basement foundation. Cars rumble along the cobblestone street, and at night, when the lamplights come on, the setting is as it was two hundred years ago. The only difference is the electrified streetlamps that were once illuminated with whale oil.*

decoration. Champagne and all the fixings for a buffet party are laid out in the sumptuous dining room. Traditionally, Dorothy is known to bake a couple of hams and provide lots of "picking" food. People flow throughout the rooms greeting one another with holiday cheer. This year the party is extra special because it not only welcomes the Christmas season, but is also a wedding celebration. Dorothy Slover and Doug Kenwood were married just an hour before the party, and invitations were verbally doled out in the same casual way that is Dorothy's style. "No gifts," she announced. "Just dress up and be at the church by five. It will be such fun." And, as always, it was.

OPPOSITE: *The rooms in this house are quite imposing, with their high ceilings, generous molding, black marble fireplace mantels, and extra-tall windows. Rose Cumming chintz is used for the deliciously extravagant draperies in the front parlor. A fire crackles in the marble fireplace, where greenery, red tulips, fresh fruit, and ribbons gracefully cascade over the mantelpiece. As a graduate of the Isabel O'Neil Studio Workshop Foundation, Dorothy is a master in the art of the painted finish. The floor cloth is an example of her fine craftsmanship.*

POINSETTIA TRIVIA

Though the poinsettia plant is indigenous to Mexico and Central America, it has become the symbol of Christmas all over the United States. These are warm-weather plants that favor moist, well-drained soil and plenty of indirect sunlight.

The name of this plant comes from an amateur botanist named Joel R. Poinsett, who helped found the National Institute for the Promotion of Science and the Useful Arts, a forerunner of the Smithsonian Institution. During the 1820s Poinsett served as a diplomat and then the first United States Minister to Mexico, where he came upon the plant. When he returned to his home in South Carolina he brought samples of the plant to grow in his greenhouse. Since poinsettias bloom in November and December and the brilliant red flowers and bright green leaves are perfect for the holiday season, it was a natural to bestow them on his friends and family at that time of year.

OPPOSITE: *A trio of figurines atop the greenery adds a personal touch. Golden balls and candy-cane-striped candles make everything sparkle.*

LEFT: *"Don't skimp on the tulips!" is Dorothy's credo when it comes to loading them onto the mantels for her once-a-year blowout Christmas party—this year a wedding celebration as well. "Lots and lots of tulips that will last for only one night seems so decadent," she says. "I love it." Lavish bows are made with yards of red- and gold-mesh ribbons tied around the lamp bases.*

BELOW: *The library is intimate and comfortably luxurious. Dorothy finished the walls to complement the leather wing chairs. The warm woods, Oriental rug, blazing fire, rich tapestries, and red Christmas accents capture the tones of the room.*

AMARYLLIS

The amaryllis is an elegant Dutch plant that
flowers the last week of November and lasts right
through New Year's Day and beyond. It is a
favorite, along with the poinsettia, as a Christmas
flower. Amaryllis has huge trumpetlike blossoms
in soft pink, white, or bright red. A bulb can
produce up to four flowers on each of two stems.
It's easy to grow because it only needs warmth,
water, and light.

*Hundreds of pink tulips have been
spread over the mantel in the grand
formal dining room. Tall amaryllis
plants march down the center of the
table laid with traditional holiday
food awaiting the guests' arrival.*

Making a Christmas Tart ➤✕◄

Making a meal, setting a table, and entertaining close friends are part of what makes the holidays a special time for most of us. If Richard Kemble and his partner, George Korn, aren't throwing a huge open house Christmas party, they are usually entertaining six in their dining room surrounded by their collection of American folk art. Friends have been invited to share a meal for this holiday, and the green-painted country table is simply set with family silverware, sparkling wineglasses, red paisley napkins, and red candlesticks.

When they bought their Victorian house on Pleasant Street it didn't need much renovation, but Kemble and Korn, who love to cook, knew they needed an updated kitchen. Today the kitchen functions just as they imagined it would. As dealers in early-American folk art and marine antiques, they have filled the house with whirligigs, old toys, weathervanes, and Nantucket-related memorabilia. Interesting artifacts from their travels, handcrafted furniture, and an eclectic collection of art adds to the character and personality of the house. Their unique decorating style is to use what they have, mix in what they find at antiques shows, flea markets, and yard sales, and add some really good art and handcrafts.

The two men are inveterate treasure hunters. On one visit George opened a box and pulled out a long panel of tapestry fabric he'd just purchased at a yard sale. "These will be fabulous on the tables at the Festival of Trees," he remarked. Richard and George co-chair the annual holiday fund-raiser.

ABOVE: *Richard's Pear Almond Tart is being prepared for the ending to a holiday dinner. The new kitchen is equipped for whipping up lots of creative meals for both intimate dinners and large Christmas parties.*

OPPOSITE: *Nakashima chairs surround the painted folk-art table set with gold charger plates, family silverware, red paisley napkins, cranberry candles, and a glass beaker filled with witch balls, originally used in early Nantucket homes for keeping evil spirits at bay. Lightship basket saltcellars by local craftsman Paul Willer and the folk-art toys and whirligigs are part of the owners' vast collection. Large red mercury balls provide a dramatic Christmas decoration over the table.*

PEAR ALMOND TART

RICHARD AND GEORGE once owned a restaurant in New Hope, Pennsylvania, and one of the many hats Richard wore was that of pastry chef. No party at their house would be complete without one of his famous desserts. For this gathering of six he made a Pear Almond Tart, a favorite holiday dessert and the perfect ending to a perfect meal.

Preheat oven to 375 degrees F. Make enough short pastry (standard pie crust) to fill a 12-inch flan ring.

SHORT PASTRY

2 cups sifted pastry flour
⅔ tsp. salt
½ cup shortening
6 tbsp. water

Sift together the flour and salt and cut in half the shortening, blending thoroughly. Add remainder of shortening and work to pebbly stage. Add water, one tablespoon at a time. Form the dough into a ball, place in a plastic bag, and chill for one hour. Roll out the dough and press into flan ring.

FILLING

¾ lb. almond paste
¾ lb. granulated sugar
5 egg whites
5 Anjou pears, peeled, cored, and halved

Mix together all ingredients except pears; pour into pastry shell.
Arrange pears, cored side down, on top of the filling. Bake for 45 minutes. Cool and remove to platter.

The pièce de résistance, and
a perfect ending to a perfect
dinner with friends.

In the Country Tradition →×←

Collecting interesting marine artifacts is a Nantucket tradition. Almost every home decor includes crafts that are indigenous to the island, such as lightship baskets and scrimshaw, and the owners often use these collectibles when decorating for the holidays. Peggy Kaufman, vice president of the Nantucket Lightship Basket Museum, likes to create holiday vignettes from her many collections of clocks, boxes, and baskets. For example, she groups her Nantucket baskets on a table in the living room and fills them with holiday plants and ornaments. Baskets of any sort can be filled in the same way; I like to put balls of green and red yarn in mine.

Peggy's collection of Raggedy Ann dolls is a favorite. They usually reside in the bedroom, but at Christmastime two or three of them sit atop an armoire in the living room, providing a childlike and playful note to the grown-up surroundings. Avoiding conventional Christmas items such as tinsel and shiny new balls, Peggy dresses her tree with ornaments she has collected over the years.

When Peggy was a public relations director for Lord and Taylor's New York department store, one of her jobs was organizing their special events, so she is no stranger to the world of entertaining. While she no longer puts on extravaganzas, she brings the same enthusiastic and creative energy to her own holiday parties, no matter how small or large.

ABOVE: *A wreath of red roses, sprigs of berries, and Christmas balls looks dramatic against the Kaufmans' colonial-blue door. The wreath, made by Flowers On Chestnut, was exhibited at the Festival of Wreaths at Preservation Hall during the Christmas Stroll weekend.*

OPPOSITE: *Painted folk-art boxes of all sizes and styles are grouped under the collection of Nantucket baskets decorated for the holidays. A painting by local artist Keith McDaniels dominates one wall of the living room.*

Peggy and her husband, Eli, host an open-house buffet party for more than a hundred people on the evening after Thanksgiving and end the season with a more intimate New Year's Eve dinner party with close friends. However, they also entertain often with ten people for dinner in their traditional dining room. Peggy sets the table with all her Nantucket country accessories and, of course, lightship baskets.

Nutcrackers are another more recent collection, and when the table is set with these playful accessories it is quite festive. The spirited marriage of all things red and green appeals to Peggy's sense of decorating a festive holiday table, and she pulls out all the stops. Her tables are set with panache and whimsy to make her guests feel celebrated. Whenever possible she integrates fresh greens and anything natural growing around her property. She shops well

LEFT: *Maria Watson designed the clever wreath made from boat rope and fishing lures to represent one of the island passions. A shelf of greens holds miniature trees above the living room windows. This is a good example of how to create a simple but elegant decorative accent in an out-of-the-way space. The wreath was created for the annual silent auction that benefits the Nantucket Historical Association.*

OPPOSITE: *Look up to find space for creating vignettes with your collectibles. A small chair, Raggedy Ann and Andy dolls, a green fern, and hand-painted blocks are arranged atop the living room armoire. Calico bows turn a plain wreath into a simple country accessory.*

A fire in the fireplace creates a warm glow throughout Peggy and Eli Kaufman's traditional dining room. The table is set for a holiday dinner party, with lightship baskets filled with pinecones, winterberries, and fresh greens alternating with cranberry candles. Dried grasses and berry twigs encircle the chandelier.

and looks for offbeat items to add to her table. "Nothing is overly expensive or precious," she says. "I like to mix and match and look for odds and ends to create a theme." She always uses place cards at her table, but in a creative way. For example, a name card might be inserted into a giant pinecone at each place setting. Once she bought a bunch of little wooden toy boats in a novelty store and wrote each person's name on one to take home after the party.

Her parties are legendary on Nantucket, and everyone always goes home with a little gift as a memento, just as they carried home "goody bags" from birthday parties when they were little. Peggy infuses her parties with sophistication, casual fun, lots of laughter, and sharing, as well as a dash of nostalgia from childhood.

ABOVE: *Artificial red Delicious apples on a bed of pine branches line the dining room mantel. Peggy topped each one with a sprig of red berries. Glass sconces at each end hold lighted candles.*

OPPOSITE: *Alternating green and red plaid place mats with green plaid napkins tucked into each wineglass create a country setting. Nutcracker ornaments and découpage plates with a fruit motif and red background add to the festive setting.*

Island Crafts

→✕← LIGHTSHIP BASKETS

Basket weaving is a time-honored craft originated by Native Americans and later taught to the first white settlers on Nantucket in the early 1600s. Like most crafts, basket weaving was born out of necessity; island Indians made and used baskets to store food and for transport.

However, the Nantucket lightship basket is different from any other basket you may have seen. These baskets, whether used as purses or to hold one egg, are considered valuable collectibles not only on the island but throughout the world. Sotheby's auction house in New York City recently auctioned off a set of nesting baskets for more than $65,000, and antiques shops all over the island routinely sell them for well into the thousands of dollars.

What makes them so valuable? Partly their history, partly the way they are made, and partly because they continue to be part of Nantucket's ongoing history related to the sea. Just as the craft of scrimshaw kept sailors busy during long stints at sea, making baskets did the same for lightship keepers. Imagine being a crewman on a Nantucket lightship anchored off Sankaty Head for eight months at a time. The ship, with two bright beacon lights and a bell that rings every two minutes during fog that can last for days, goes nowhere. It is a dangerous job because in storms the lightship could break loose from its moorings or, worse, possibly be rammed by another vessel. It was one of the loneliest jobs, with many long, monotonous hours, and so, in an effort to stave off the boredom as well as to be productive, the inventive lightship keepers made baskets.

The first baskets, made on board the *South Shoal Lightship*, were constructed of tightly woven staves or ribs of white-oak cane with an oak rim, handle, and bottom. This type of basket dates from at least the mid-1800s, when molds were first brought onto the lightship. By the 1860s there were a

A collection of scrimshaw and lightship baskets in varying sizes are clustered on a side table. Tartan-plaid ribbon dresses up the breadbasket holding bright red apples. White poinsettia plants were chosen over traditional red ones because they go so well with the color of the scrimshaw whale tooth and ivory carvings on the baskets.

considerable number of baskets being made. While it is believed that the baskets were made as early as the 1820s, it wasn't until they were made on lightships for some time that they were officially named a Nantucket lightship basket.

How a Basket Is Made

Simply described, a basket is woven over a mold. Every basket maker uses his or her own, slightly different molds, and it is this that differentiates one artisan's baskets from another's. The round bottom, which is turned on a wood lathe, is usually made of oak, although some contemporary baskets have a cherrywood bottom. The oval bottom is cut with a jigsaw. A slot cut around the edge of the bottom receives the staves of the basket. The bottom is then screwed onto a mold made in the form of the basket. The staves of the basket are made by splitting a wedge of oak or hickory into thin strips in lengths and widths depending on the size of the basket and tapered so they are smaller at the bottom and usually beveled. After the staves are softened in water, they are placed in the slot on the bottom and bent to fit the mold, then held in place with a cord. When dry, they take on the shape of the basket mold. A thin strip of cane, softened in the same way, is woven around the staves until it is completed. The basket is finished with a rim of two hoops of half-round oak strips that are riveted to the top of the staves and then wrapped with cane. Handles are also unique to each basket maker. Some are quite thin and delicate, others flat and a bit wider. The handles are often fastened with rivets, or pins, and many have ivory knobs.

The original baskets were made in sizes ranging from a pint to a peck and a half. To conserve space on board ship the sailors wove baskets in concentric sizes so they could nest neatly inside one another. Nantucket lightship purses were introduced in 1945 by a weaver named Jose Reyes, who moved to the island from the Philippines. These "friendship baskets" quickly became the most fashionable accessory carried by island women and are still popular today. The purse is oval with a wooden lid, usually adorned with a carved piece of ivory or scrimshaw. Nowadays there are many different sizes and shapes of purses, and prices vary with style and craftsmanship.

Education is key when buying a basket. The Nantucket Lightship Basket Museum on Union Street displays many antique and contemporary baskets as well as a video of baskets being made. This delightful museum also houses a replica of Jose Reyes's early workshop with baskets at various stages of construction.

⇥⤨⇤ SCRIMSHAW

Scrimshaw is the art of scribing a design on a piece of ivory or bone. A design is drawn or traced onto the material, then scribed by penetrating the surface with a sharp instrument such as an X-Acto knife, dental tool, or intaglio point, a common scribing tool found in art-supply stores. Once the design is scribed it is covered with India ink or watercolor dye. When wiped away from the surface of the material, the ink that has settled into the incised lines makes a permanent design.

Scrimshaw, one of our first American folk crafts, originated during our nation's earliest years with New England whalers who spent several years at sea. To relieve the boredom, these sailors spent their leisure time drawing and scribing on whale teeth and bone. Some of the most popular early items were tool handles, clothespins, walking sticks, jagging wheels, and busks to stiffen a woman's corset. Although many sailors were fine draftsmen, most of the early scrimshanders (as one who practices this craft is called) were not artists, so they either produced fairly crude drawings or traced designs from magazines of the day. Today's scrimshanders are talented artists who are still doing pretty much what the old scrimshander did, only better. They have adapted nautical themes from the past as well as taking advantage of the use of colored dyes to expand the design potential. The modern pieces of jewelry often incorporate colorful wildflowers as well as nautical scenes.

Because no more whaling is done in this country, the availability of whale teeth is limited to what is left from many years ago, when supplies were imported from other countries. This is no longer legal, and as the supply dwindles, scrimshanders are turning to substitute materials such as bone and resin.

Dining Out for Christmas →✕←

The Company of the Cauldron is an intimate little restaurant housed in a delightfully charming old building in the middle of town. The chef-proprietors, All and Andrea Kovalencik, offer a single prix-fixe menu that changes daily. Andrea says, "We want our guests to feel as though they are at a dinner party. The atmosphere is cozy in a communal setting." Several nights a week dinner is accompanied by the classical harp music of Mary Keller.

During the holiday season Andrea decorates the restaurant with garlands of pine branches and pinecones over the front windows that face India Street. Urns are filled with bright red poinsettia plants, and baskets or tins are filled with silver and red glass balls. Strands of cranberries drape across the windows like jeweled necklaces. The warm woods and simple decor create a convivial and relaxed atmosphere, making patrons feel like they are in a friend's dining room.

RIGHT: *All Kovalencik, chef and owner of the Company of the Cauldron, a restaurant in the heart of Nantucket, serves one of his holiday specialties: rack of lamb with cranberry Israeli couscous and grilled asparagus, garnished with fresh herbs and kumquats and accompanied by a hearty red wine and locally baked bread.*

During the Christmas season Andrea Kovalencik decorates with bowers of greens and red poinsettia plants. A single pine sprig adorns each table. The painting of the front of the restaurant was a gift from a patron.

OPPOSITE: *Occasionally during the two seatings each night, dinner is accompanied by classical harp music provided by Mary Keller.*

When setting a table for the holidays, pull out all the stops. I like to combine all my favorite things—vintage champagne glasses, ornate silverware, silk place mats, my grandmother's silver candlesticks, and lots of candles. While the tree is always covered with silver, gold, and bronze ornaments, the rest of the house is predominantly red at Christmastime.

111

Ready to Entertain

Dressing Up for the Holidays! →×←

Nantucket has been my home for over twenty years. "What do you do there in the winter?" I am often asked by a summer visitor. "Probably exactly what you do where you live" is my usual answer. However, living on an island is different. You cannot suddenly decide to go somewhere without careful planning. Traveling by boat or plane when a change of scenery is desired is part of island life. Like most people who live here, I chose to make Nantucket my home and I love everything about it—from the isolation of living on an island to the connectedness of a close-knit community. My husband and partner, Jon Aron, a graphic designer and photographer, and I live in the historic district on the corner of two of the prettiest streets in town, Flora and Union. While the outside of the house conforms to the guidelines set forth by the Nantucket Historic District Commission, the inside is contemporary for the location. Out-of-town houses have more architectural leeway.

By the first of November I'm eager to fill my own house with all the decorations to welcome the holidays. I start decorating for Christmas before Thanksgiving because I love the smell of the tree in the house and I want to enjoy all the Christmas ornaments and things I've collected for many years for as long as possible. Since my business is writing about home style, decorating, and crafts with a leaning toward do-it-yourself, creating holiday pieces starts in the summertime. I make what I write about, and my studio is next door to my office, so I spend time running between the two.

Over the years I've had the opportunity to see many amazingly beautiful homes on the island. While I always favor those that are minimally decorated, with more elegance than glitz, when it comes to Christmas I confess to having no restraint and give myself permission to be extravagantly exuberant for this very brief period of time. By New Year's Day I'm quite sated and ready to put everything away and pare down to all white.

Every year, Jon and I go to London early in November to buy for the shop that we own in town. My specialty is découpage and I buy early botanical prints for the plates I make. The stores are filled with unusual Christmas offerings not always available at home, so I end up bringing back decorations as well. I especially favor a glittering tree, and in this regard I

I set my table with the series of découpage Christmas plates I make for my store. Nantucket artist Barbara Van Winkelen creates the original artwork, and we collaborate on this limited-edition project. The gold marbleized background against hunter green and the gold rim on the plates make it a festive choice for a holiday dinner. Early champagne glasses hold floating candles, and silver- and gold-coated almonds are strewn across the table.

I bring out everything red for my living room decorations. A favorite early patchwork quilt is thrown over the white love seat, and I cover occasional pillows with red plaid fabric. My red-painted table holds a lamp and découpaged platter with a sprig of holly; a milk-glass bowl holds a red pomegranate and green apples. The wire basket on the coffee table holds tiny crabapples, always a good prop, and underneath, a pewter bowl holds balls of red yarn. The large red velvet poinsettias in a brown vase fill the corner of the room. I also pile all my books with red or green covers under the coffee table and wherever they look good. There is nothing more inviting than a bowl of red and green candies somewhere in the room.

look for silver, gold, and bronze ornaments, both old and new. There are never fewer than 400 lights on our tree, and more always seems better.

For the table and the rest of the house I take out everything red that I own. I have a red Oriental carpet in the living room, so everything follows this color scheme and works well with my white walls, warm woods, and soft furnishings. Greens punctuate the Christmas decor.

Preparations for entertaining begin the day before a party is planned, giving me plenty of time to set a festive table. I love to use all my favorite things in creative ways, mixing the old and cherished with the newly acquired. The dining table is ample and I cover it with everything I can reasonably rationalize putting on it.

This year I set the table with the découpaged Christmas plates that I make for the store. There are eight different original wreath designs that are part of my limited-edition series. I have a large collection of napkins and place mats, and for this setting I chose the green and red silk with gold trim to go with the plates and the green and red chargers. My traditional silverware is ornate, and I think this is what silverware should be. It dresses up any table.

Lots and lots of candles at different heights provide enough lighting for romantic dining without room lights, and I use all sorts of holders, from art deco champagne glasses holding gold floating candles to my grandmother's silver candlesticks holding red tapers. The table is dotted with silver and gold tree balls I've owned for years and tiny golden balls I bought recently. Red-plaid napkins (always linen!) are held with beaded satin silver napkin rings, and the table is strewn with silver and gold almond candies from London. Five miniature live trees in terra-cotta pots (from Flowers On Chestnut, see page 161) march down the center of the table. At other times I fill a cut-glass vase (once my mother's) with red cranberries to hold a bouquet of red tulips (see page 117). Pure white calla lilies are another favorite floral choice. I always drop a few cranberries into the champagne glasses just before filling them, welcoming any opportunity to add just one more touch of red!

CRANBERRIES

Nantucket has actively cultivated cranberries since 1857. The largest bog is 234 acres located off the Milestone Road, midway between town and Siasconset ('Sconset for short), and there is another 40-acre bog on Polpis Road, owned by the Nantucket Conservation Foundation and operated by Northland Cranberries, Inc. During the fall and winter months, islanders use cranberries in recipes and for crafting holiday decorations.

Pollinated by bees, cranberry flowers develop into fruit that is harvested during the early fall. The berries are shipped to the mainland to be processed into juice and other cranberry products. Each year islanders gather to celebrate the arrival of fall and to watch the harvesting of the cranberries.

LEFT: *A worker herds the berries by walking through the shallow bog and pulling them in to shore.*

ABOVE: *Michael Molinar, owner of Flowers On Chestnut, has a creative use for cranberries. He fills a vase with the crimson fruit, adds water, then an abundance of red and white tulips, for a holiday display on a coffee table in Judy and Bob Seinfeld's house (see page 180). A handcrafted pillow and starfish ornament add playful touches.*

4   *Personal Pleasures*

More Is More ⇥⇤

"Red, red, red, I love it," says Thomas Koon. "I always use red. I love decorating with red. I don't think a house is complete without red." Thom and his partner, Bart Cosgrove, have a delightful house on the edge of town. Tucked away in the woods, the house is reached by a winding dirt road leading to a little island within an island. The small house is chock-a-block with treasures culled from the owners' many travels around the world. Everything has a story, and Thom loves to tell about how they acquired every single possession. Christmas is a special time here, and the two men go all the way, decorating every inch of their space inside and out. "I love taking out things and changing the spaces because I love touching things and remembering where they came from," Thom says as he points out the hanging lanterns. "I bought them in the Paris shop in Las Vegas because they're so Moroccan."

PREVIOUS SPREAD: *The holiday anticipation starts at the front door, where the homeowners like to be creative with their lighting decor. This year blue and purple lights cast a romantic aura over the front porch.*

OPPOSITE: *Shelves in the dining room hold collections of red chinaware, and at Christmastime the owners drape red and purple beads over all for a bejeweled setting fit for a palace.*

ABOVE: *The dining table is set with a regal red and purple theme. The purple velvet runner is festooned with lots of candles, red glasses, purple and blue Christmas balls, and garlands of golden glitter. Red chargers hold the Limoges plates edged with gold, and red linen napkins are placed on top of each setting. Everything sparkles.*

At Christmastime these homeowners feel that more is definitely better. "You can't overdo it," Thom emphasizes. He changes the decor every year depending on mood, but at Christmastime everything comes out. Their home has one little surprise after another.

Aside from their travel possessions, the house is filled with paintings by local Nantucket artists: William Welsh, the late Irmgard Arvin and Bobby Bushong, James Harrington, Laura Lovitt, Loretta Daminowski, Peter Guarino, Maggie Meredith, David Brenizer, David Cross, and Jacqueline Vermiliea, to name a few. Avid fans of the Broadway musical, Thom and Bart play show tunes all day and into the evening. Compact discs of every show they've seen are alphabetically catalogued and stored in a unique display around the rafters of the living room.

Mercury glass and silver, a candelabra from the Nantucket Looms, monkey ornaments from Italy, a jewel box, Limoges plates from a shop in Paris, and anything purple and

ABOVE, TOP: *King Tut was won at a local auction and opens to reveal shelves holding more collectibles. He is the perfect silent butler, watching over guests who come to dine here in splendor. On cold winter nights Thom makes his famous chili dish for his close friends, who enjoy partaking of this homey comfort food in such an elegant setting.*

ABOVE, BOTTOM: *Paintings by Nantucket artists, family photographs, a wooden crèche, a vase of red roses, and votive candles sprinkled throughout make a corner of the living room warm and inviting. The elephant pillow was purchased on a trip to Paris.*

OPPOSITE: *The mantel in the living room is the perfect stage for a holiday setting. Fresh boughs of pine dotted with lavishly jeweled balls, candles at different heights, and baubles and collectibles reflect the owners' personal tastes. A tin angel is centered over the mosaic tile surround on the warm wood of the fireplace. Every square inch is carefully arranged for visual enjoyment. The hooked rug reflects all the colors in the room.*

*The old glass panes of
the window reflect the
candlelight, doubling
the impact of this mantel
display. Candlesticks laden
with ornaments, a glass
vase filled with green and
red balls, and greens dotted
with holly berries and
a variety of ornaments
create a lavish scene.*

red are all part of the extravaganza Koon and Cosgrove orchestrate for Christmas. And the interior is just the beginning. Outside on the deck the trees are carefully choreographed with lights to create an environment that can only be described as enchanting. In front of the house the lights on the trees welcome visitors and draw them to the enchantment that awaits within. The table is set for a party that is always about to take place. When Thom is asked the best way to pour champagne, he doesn't hesitate to answer, "To the top." This house makes magic.

ABOVE: *A picture window with a deep ledge holds more glittery collections: a silver mercury-glass lamp, hanging Moroccan lanterns, glass balls shaped like teardrops, silver balls on top of greens spiked with acorns collected around the grounds, all displayed against a backdrop of purple lights on the trees outside.*

OPPOSITE: *A chandelier at one end of the living room is festooned with beaded harlequin balls and dancing-monkey ornaments.*

Peaceable Kingdom ⇥⇤

Glenora Kelly-Smith loves Christmas more than any other time of the year. "To me, Christmas is about giving, not getting," she says. She proves this throughout the year as she plans, designs, and crafts all sorts of decorations and gifts for friends and extended family. Over the years this fiber artist has made petit-point heart ornaments for all the people or landmarks in her life, and she puts a lot of thought, love, and often humor into each very personal design. When her children were little she made up all sorts of fairytales and planned wonderfully imaginative parties for them. "On Christmas Eve," she says, "we used to write a note to Santa and let it go up the chimney. Then when they were asleep I would put my boots in the fireplace ashes and make footprints on the floor leading from the fireplace to the milk and cookies." Glenora goes the extra mile to create a fantasy for the people she cares about. Whether she's decorating for the holidays, knitting a sweater, making petit-point stockings and ornaments, writing poetry, or planting her garden, it is done with unusual care and creativity. When you enter her home you are instantly in Glenora's world of imagination and beauty. She uses handsome branches or materials found in the woods around her house to recycle into romantic decorations.

OPPOSITE: *Subtle colors and textures of stone, marble, wood, tapestry, silk, and mohair mix together to create an inviting living-room sanctuary. The fireplace is encircled with a bough of greens holding needlepoint ornaments that relate to all the people and important landmarks in Glenora Kelly-Smith's life. Two green pails hold narcissus on either side of the hearth.*

RIGHT: *Glenora designs and makes the stockings and ornaments depicting personal scenes, favorite events that uniquely represent her friends and members of her family. Each ornament has bits and pieces of memorabilia and whimsy woven into the tapestry.*

The house that Glenora designed and built is far from town in what Nantucketers call the country. It is in an area known as Fulling Mill, where sheep were raised and shorn when farming was an industry here. A painting of what the area looked like back then hangs in her living room. To reach the house one must drive past the old Life Saving Museum, down a winding dirt road lined with pine trees, and, in winter, over many ruts and potholes. But once you're around the curves and over the bumps you arrive at Glenora's enchanted cottage in the woods. The furnishings are soft and tactile, and the house is filled with light. The adobe-style fireplace is the focal point of the living room; to sit here by the fire watching the snow falling on the pine trees surrounding the house is magical. The balcony overlooking the living room is Glenora's studio, where she designs and creates her whimsical projects and does her writing.

This Christmas she is making three new petit-point ornaments. She uses bits of memorabilia such as old school ties, lavender and lace, parts of worn quilts, antique charms, and bits and pieces of things she's collected to personalize her art.

The collection she is most proud of is "The Peaceable Kingdom," with all the representative animals of all the continents. She arranges them each Christmas on a large table in the greenhouse that serves as her dining room. Although her son and daughter are married and living off-island, they always try to get together for the holidays. Glenora still decorates and celebrates Christmas with the same childlike enthusiasm she did when they were little, because, as she says, "I'm still a child at heart."

OPPOSITE, TOP: *The greenhouse becomes an enchantingly romantic setting for dining when the snow covers the ground and falls on the glass rooftop. Candles provide the only light. When it's not used for dining, Glenora arranges "The Peaceable Kingdom" she's created on a linen tablecloth draped as if it were a blanket of snow. Her creation is based on the seven continents of the world: a unicorn from Europe, a tiger from Asia, a lion representing Africa, an ox for North America, a penguin from the Antarctic, a wooly ram from South America, a koala bear from Australia, and a polar bear from the Arctic, all surrounding the baby in a manger. Miniature topiary trees and candelabras surround the table at jaunty angles and complete the scene.*

LEFT: *Glenora made a needlepoint figure of Father Christmas complete with his fluffy beard, knit scarf, and hat, holding a bag of toys. She then created a scene with the animals and moss-covered miniature lighted tree on the marble table in front of the curved windows in her living room.*

An Artist in Residence ►►◄◄

Joan Albaugh has a gift for the lighthearted, impromptu, amusing, beckoning, and whimsical. A winding path leads to the simple Cape Cod shingled house nestled in a grove of pine trees. Nothing on the outside prepares you for the irreverent environment this artist has created inside. Joan lives here with her teenage son, Jack, and the two share a quirky passion for collecting almost anything vintage. There are metal lunchboxes hanging from the kitchen rafters, salt and pepper shakers on the windowsills, marionettes suspended in limbo, nutcrackers, tin candy boxes, a slew of Pez dispensers, and her paintings all around the rooms. This offbeat designer has created visual excitement wherever you look. She says, "It doesn't matter how much space I have. I'll always fill it up." At Christmastime, Joan invokes the spirit of holidays gone by with greenery cut from the woods around her house and things that hold sentimental value to her.

Joan Albaugh is a landscape artist who paints in oils and is represented by the Old Spouter Gallery (see page 138). Her work is often described as a mix between Edward Hopper's and Grant Wood's, but she refers to her paintings as isolated landscapes caught in time. "My paintings are a bit nostalgic. I create little still-life scenes on my tabletops in the same way." There's an element of whimsy in Joan's arrangements—monkeys with hats sit on a sofa or chair or perch on a window ledge; doll heads that survived their bodies are given Santa hats and lined up on the mantel. Nothing gets thrown away. There is also another

OPPOSITE: *Artist Joan Albaugh fills her house with vintage collections that bring back fond memories of childhood. Her tree is covered with old and new ornaments and many that she and her son, Jack, have made over the years.*

ABOVE: *Handmade stockings for adults and cats hang on the fire screen, and all sorts of monkeys and surviving parts of childhood dolls are surrounded by fresh greens on the mantel. One of Joan's landscapes hangs over the fireplace.*

The house is decorated with greens cut from the yard, collectibles from childhood, including the dollhouse with Santa and reindeer on the roof, handmade stockings, hanging marionettes, and antique furniture from Joan's family. Her oil paintings fill the walls.

Joan uses every occasion to bake a creative theme cake. For Christmas she makes a layer cake to resemble a ski slope and decorates it with miniature trees, reindeer, elves, skiers, and a sleigh rider. Coconut is used as snow, and miniature nonpareils surround the bottom layer.

135
→►◄←
*Personal
Pleasures*

collection of snow domes from all different places. And while she's always been drawn to painting houses, she also collects dollhouses from her childhood. Christmas is an excuse to enhance her collections by dressing them up with greens and baubles.

The Christmas tree is covered with a variety of worn vintage glass ornaments that suggest years of loving use. She points out the "shiny brights"—large, garish ornaments from the 1950s mixed with some recently acquired reissued copies. There are also a number of ornaments made by Joan and her son. One does not expect tiny, clear fairy lights on Joan's tree; it is lit with the big old-fashioned bulbs in primary colors.

"Growing up," Joan says, "I always had three trees, a large one in the living room and two on each side of the fireplace, Santas and folk art and lots of vintage stuff. I inherited some Victorian things from my grandmother when I was in college and that started my serious collecting." Her grandmother traveled a lot and always brought back a doll from each country she visited. This evolved into a very large collection that is now housed in a china cabinet, one of the antique pieces of furniture from her childhood.

VINTAGE COLLECTING

Vintage ornaments and all things related to the holidays are becoming highly collectible. Early cookie jars, for example, are fun and whimsical and always give off good feelings when displayed in a corner of the kitchen. Filled with homemade cookies, they make a great gift.

Vintage cookie jars were known as art pottery. In 1939 the Abingdon Company issued its first "Little Old Lady" jar. After World War I, McCoy and Bisque were known names in collectible pottery. Old Christmas jars included figures of Santa, Rudolph, snowmen, trees, gingerbread men and women, toy soldiers, trains, and circus and nursery-rhyme characters.

Cardboard candy containers made between 1870 and 1930 designed as tree ornaments were part of the treats children might receive at a Sunday school pageant. The most popular designs featured a Santa or a Christmas scene, and they had string handles for hanging on the tree.

Pint-size brush trees were made in Japan through the 1940s. Turkey-feather trees were made in Germany through the 1930s.

OPPOSITE: *The newly added dining room is painted in an unconventional lavender to offset the dark woods, collections, and paintings. The china cabinet houses a doll collection, and Joan has created a winter wonderland scene in the middle of the table. Island friends will gather here for an eggnog get-together.*

ABOVE: *A miniature outdoor scene fills the dining room table. Skaters glide on a mirrored glass "pond" in the middle of white, fluffy "snow." The pinecone tree covered with balls and packages came from Joan's grandmother. Joan spray-painted branches from her yard silver and surrounded the perimeter with elves, reindeer, angels, trees, and garlands of beads. The snow globe is a favorite from her collection.*

Childhood Memories ⇥⤝

Kathleen Walsh and Brent Young live in a modern apartment that is furnished in the old-world style of an Italian palazzo, with antiques, velvet drapes, brocade fabrics, leather sofas, antique furniture, and accessories with a past. Kathleen is the owner of the Old Spouter Gallery, housed below the apartment, where she represents most of Nantucket's better-known artists, including Joan Albaugh (see "An Artist in Residence," page 133). Her husband, Brent, is a builder on the island and is responsible for the renovation of the apartment as well as of many of Nantucket's finest older homes (see "In the Holiday Spirit," page 180).

When it comes to celebrating the holidays, Kathleen and Brent pull out all the stops. The couple look for the tallest tree they can find and cover it with ornaments that Kathleen has collected since childhood. Christmas is a special time for them and the tree is always loaded with meaningful decorations. As she removes tissue and wrappings from each item that has been carefully packed away in the seventeenth-

ABOVE, TOP: *The angel painting* State of Grace *by Kathleen Walsh's sister, Deidre Briggs, is the main feature of the entryway. A pine table is decked out with vintage holiday ornaments, and a silver bowl is filled with candies for guests to help themselves to when coming and going.*

ABOVE, BOTTOM: *The bears in the sleigh were a gift from her dad when Kathleen was a child, and they take center stage under the tree each year.*

OPPOSITE: *Velvet drapes frame the large windows that allow the lighted tree to be seen from outdoors. The tree, covered with meaningful ornaments from Kathleen's childhood, dominates one end of the living room. Deidre Briggs made Cymbeline, the Christmas jester seen next to Father Christmas holding a baby lamb under the tree. Kathleen's brother David made the coffee table from a street grate.*

century Italian trunk (once a marriage coffer), she is reminded of past Christmases or memorable moments in her life. Every year her collection grows with new pieces she acquires.

The trees surrounding their property are lighted, not in the traditional colors but rather more creatively with burnt-orange lights, much like the color of bronze ornamentation one might find in medieval times. Located on busy Orange Street, one of the island's main roads in and out of town, it is a lovely sight for all those driving by at dusk. An oversize wreath hangs on the side of the gallery encircling the name, and when there's a holiday art exhibit a blackboard announces "Art Opening Tonight." It is a seasonal event that no one wants to miss.

Aside from the classic glass balls, there are all sorts of molded shapes on Brent and Kathleen's tree. The soft-sculpture lion with his "Courage" badge from The Wizard of Oz *is one of their favorites.*

VINTAGE ORNAMENTS

The golden age of Christmas ornaments dates between 1930 and 1940. Glass ornaments like the pinecone were often hung on trees, along with real ones. Glass Santa heads were made in the 1930s from a clay or wooden mold, but the Santa doll head with the cone hat was probably from a later era. In the 1880s Woolworth's sold imported ornaments from Germany for reasonable prices. Many of these extremely fragile pieces are still intact, as they were carefully packed away most of the year, now considered to have become very collectible. Newer versions were made to look like the earlier ones, but the glass is much lighter.

Eggshell-thin, mold-blown silver and gold glass ornaments of detailed figures, fruits, and animals were very popular in the early 1900s. Before 1940 these ornaments, mostly from Germany, were mouth-blown, then silvered, dyed, and decorated by hand and topped with a tin or steel cap.

Wax angels were also imported from Germany before 1929. They were popular items in the 1926 Sears, Roebuck catalog.

LEFT: *Every Christmas Kathleen and Brent host a holiday drop-in for their friends and the artists represented in their gallery. Brent sets up his Lionel trains on the large oval table between the living room and kitchen. One boxcar holds a group of tiny angels; another is filled with red and green M&M's. All sorts of platters of food fill the center of the table while the train chugs merrily around the edge. Kathleen uses her dad's bejeweled box creations to hold napkins and silverware. Each box is decorated with a variety of ornate found gems, beads, grommets, and all sorts of wonderful doodads. They fit perfectly into this old-world setting.*

ABOVE: *Kathleen's dad, David Walsh II, made the jewel-encrusted gift boxes on each end of the mantel. The miniature village is one of her prized possessions and becomes part of her Christmas decorating tradition each year.*

OPPOSITE: *The fireplace surround was found at a local antiques shop, and Brent built the fireplace at one end of the living room to fit the mantel. The silk crazy-quilt runner with fur tassels is spread across the mantel. It is quite fragile and comes out only once a year. A painted Swedish village is arranged on top, along with miniature sheep and pine trees.* The Lamb's Dream, *featuring the dove of peace, is a painting by Deidre Briggs.*

ABOVE: *Nantucket Harbor, seen in the distance from the living room window, provides the perfect setting for another display. Incense drapes nicely over the windowsill along with fresh pine branches. Potted topiaries are set in rugged terra-cotta pots, and lighted candles are reflected in the windowpanes. When Kathleen was sixteen her dad gave her the wooden horse-drawn carriage that is a replica of a coach from the late 1600s.*

Santa's Workshop →×←

Right after Thanksgiving Jackie Peterson sets up her Santa's Workshop in her country dining room, where it stays on view until New Year's Day. Many years ago Jackie took a course with a group of women to learn how to create a miniature version of Santa's Workshop. Each person created her own rendition, and over the years Jackie has added numerous items that she's collected from church bazaars, craft fairs, and gifts that friends have given her. Santa's Nantucket Workshop has grown and provides a constant source of creative enjoyment as Jackie continues to look for and make tiny items to add to her original creation. A project like this can, over the years, be expanded to become a work of art. What a wonderful heirloom to pass on to future generations!

ABOVE, TOP: *To make her Santa's Workshop, Jackie Peterson started with a simple wooden box. All the woodwork was first cut and stained, then painted. The sections of the bay window were glued in place, after which each crosspiece was assembled. Next, the working Dutch door was put together. The snow on the roof is made of Spackle, and the icicles are made from silicone gel.*

ABOVE, BOTTOM: *The front of the workshop is removed to reveal a fantasy environment where Santa resides with his elves. Once the basic furniture was in place, Jackie discovered that there's no end to what can be done. "You simply can't overdo it," she says. Shops devoted to dollhouse furniture provided all sorts of accessories, such as the tiny skis propped in one corner.*

OPPOSITE, TOP: *Santa's tree is wrapped with a garland made from packing popcorn. The candy canes are made from red and white telephone wire, and a miniature calendar by Tasha Tudor hangs on the wall. A crochet wreath adorns the fireplace, and Jackie made the stocking from a scrap of red fabric. The tree and the fireplace light up.*

OPPOSITE, BOTTOM: *One of Santa's elves sits on a miniature newspaper surrounded by tiny toys and the tools used to make them.*

Harbor Lights →><←

Old North Wharf, Nantucket's second-oldest wharf, built in 1750, juts out into Nantucket Harbor. Today it is lined on both sides with modest structures that were originally built as fishing shacks and boat shops. In the early 1900s these shacks were used to cull and prepare quahogs to be shipped to the mainland. Each building is named after a whale ship, all once owned by Jared Coffin. The wharf was designated an historic district in 1955. Over the years many of these buildings were sold and transformed into charming little houses, which the current owners often refer to as boathouses. Vacationers and boat owners use them mostly in the summer months; however, a few of them are lived in year-round.

One of the larger houses, by Old North Wharf standards, is a delightful cottage decorated with all sorts of fun accessories found in island shops. The lady of the house, Antje Farber, has furnished it with a decidedly Scandinavian feeling to reflect her background. Painted cottage furniture blends nicely with deep, comfortable chairs and sofas that fill the small rooms with coziness and charm. The pine-paneled walls create an old-fashioned, cabinlike feeling. Everything from the rafters to the mantel to the canopy bed to the outdoor railings is decked out with greens and bows and hundreds of twinkling lights for the holiday season. While she spends most of the year in Florida, Antje likes to come here for a little Christmas

OPPOSITE: *Old North Wharf cottage decked out for Christmas. From the rooftop deck one can watch the incoming boats rounding Brant Point.*

ABOVE: *The Christmas flag waves above the upstairs deck. The railing is wrapped with greens and lots and lots of tiny clear glass lights. The bedroom doors open onto the deck, where one can see far across the harbor.*

149
→><←
Personal Pleasures

getaway. She says she loves this house as much when the wind howls outside, snowflakes fall, and the foghorn bellows from Brant Point Lighthouse outside the windows as she does in the middle of summer when their boat is tied up to a pier just steps from their front door.

Taking advantage of the location is not difficult when it comes to decorating for Christmas. Scallop-shell lights outline doorways front and back, island greens and berry branches fill the quaint window boxes, and wreaths are hung in as many places as possible. Even the stone dogs standing guard at the front door are treated to wreath collars. There can never be too many fairy lights as far as Antje is concerned. When these houses are lit up it is a lovely and welcoming sight for passengers coming to the island by ferry from the mainland.

A Nantucket
Christmas

ABOVE, TOP: *Red winter jackets hanging in the front hall, apples on the greens, and a red bow on the front door wreath welcome in the season. In summer the owners have only to walk out their front door to step onto their boat tied to a pier in the harbor. All the comings and goings by water can be witnessed from this vantage point.*

ABOVE, BOTTOM: *Wicker baskets filled with greens, birdhouses galore, and the Christmas wreath on the side door are covered with snow after a surprise storm. Nantucket is typically milder than the mainland because of the Gulf Stream. When the rare snowstorm hits, the island is turned into a winter wonderland at sea, making it all the more romantic.*

OPPOSITE: *Scallop-shell lights, island greens, and berries decorate the front of the cottage. Even the stone dogs are outfitted in holiday finery to greet visitors.*

RIGHT: *A lavish garland of sugared fruit, pinecones, ribbons, greens, and tassels accentuates the doorway, over which hangs a painting of Brant Point and Sankaty Lighthouses and sailboats in the harbor on a less blustery day.*

BELOW: *A Christmas tree fills the corner of the open room. The tree is covered with needlepoint and cross-stitch ornaments, little felt trees covered with buttons, as well as nautical baubles such as lighthouses, fishing lures, miniature lobster traps, and painted scallop shells filling the branches. Scallop-shell lights and garlands of beads add the finishing touches.*

LEFT: *A painted table is set for a Christmas-morning breakfast. The furnishings, paintings, and decorations reflect the owner's Scandinavian background. The glass compote filled with red and green polished apples makes a natural centerpiece. Nothing detracts from the views. Simple ornaments hanging in the windows and from a valance at the top are all that's needed.*

ABOVE: *The canopy bed in the master bedroom is wrapped with greens, pillows are dressed in their Christmas covers, and tea is served elegantly in George Davis's Wedgwood Nantucket Basket china (see page 169). A special early-morning present is tucked into the lace-edged napkin. As the snow falls, nowhere is cozier than under the sumptuous duvet.*

HYDRANGEA WREATHS

In the summertime hydrangea bushes bloom all over the island. These big, beautiful, blue, pink, lavender, and wine-colored blossoms are a sight to behold. Not wanting to relegate them to summer enjoyment alone, the crafty islanders have found a way to enjoy them all year long. Early in the fall, when the blossoms are just past their prime, they are picked and used to make holiday wreaths. While many people make these wreaths, JoAnn Johnson has turned it into an artful business. Her lovely creations are made and offered for sale from her flower truck, which parks on Main Street each morning in early fall.

The wreaths can be hung in windows or on a protected door, or you might like to use them as a centerpiece with a grouping of candles in the middle. Some of the hydrangeas dry to silvery blue, while others turn pale green or retain their deep wine color.

It is easy to make your own wreath if you have a hydrangea bush in your yard. All you need are a Styrofoam or straw wreath-form, florist's pins and wire, and a pair of small clippers. If the straw wreath-form is in cellophane, leave it wrapped, as this will keep it from shedding. You can use flowers of the same color or vary them depending on the blossoms you find. Use blossoms that are about the size of a fist. Remove any brown petals.

Many people like the classic holiday look of a hydrangea wreath on the front door. It is a reminder of summer and the beautiful blossoms found all over the island.

MAKING A HYDRANGEA WREATH

1. *Make a wreath hanger by wrapping a piece of wire around the wreath-form and twisting it into a loop at the top.*

2. *Hold the blossom in one hand and scrunch it up so the stem is exposed.*

3. *Place the blossom on the wreath-form and pin it in position with a florist's pin. Clip the excess end of the stem.*

4. *Continue to add blossoms to the wreath as tightly packed together as possible.*

5 *Celebrating in Style*

Pure and Simple ⇥⇤

Michael Molinar has owned Flowers On Chestnut, a flower and gift shop where he has sold unique home accessories, for more than twenty years. He is responsible for many of the holiday decorations and floral arrangements found in the houses throughout this book. His loyal following would not dream of throwing a party, having houseguests, planning a wedding, or moving into a new house without consulting him first. "The best thing about my job," Michael says, "is that I never get tired of going into houses. My favorite thing is when a customer calls to say she has moved into a new house and asks me to come over. We walk through the rooms and she (sometimes he) will ask me what kinds of flowers I would suggest and where they should go. I get to know their style of decorating and entertaining and can keep the rooms looking fresh all season with just the right arrangements. I love all sorts of houses on the island and I'm lucky to get invited into so many of them."

ABOVE: *White amaryllis, tulips, and candles in glass candlesticks dress up the snowy-white living room. Paintings by Michael Haykin, John Osborne, and other local artists are hung together on one wall for impact. The paintings add just enough color and interest to suit the owner, who favors a spare environment. The elevated tree covered with ornaments and a bevy of identically wrapped gifts welcome in the season. "This year was easy," Michael says. "I found the perfect gift for everyone on my list."*

OPPOSITE: *A simple boxwood wreath and red velvet bow hang on the front door of Michael Molinar's newly renovated 1800s house. Greens and winterberries fill window boxes on the front porch and under the front windows.*

At Christmastime the second floor of the shop looks like Santa's workshop, brimming with the most beautiful wrappings, ribbons, and ornaments to dress up the prettiest homes on the island. I thought it would be fun to go behind the scenes of one of the island's creative people to see how he makes things for others and how he decorates his own house.

Michael lives in an in-town house built in 1835. It was neglected, in need of total rehabilitation, and he has done it with incredible restraint and without altering the original proportions of the rooms. Only a wall in the kitchen was removed. The floorboards still slant and the doorways are narrow, making it seem cozy and charmingly quaint. "Something about this place caught my imagination," he says. "I love old houses, so long as there are modern amenities, like a grown-up bathroom and a well-functioning kitchen."

When it comes to decorating, Michael is a minimalist and favors an all-white scheme combined with warmth coming from the natural wood tones of the furniture. A master at

OPPOSITE: *The dining area is an extension of the kitchen. Michael likes a pared-down expression of holiday decorations and is known for his signature statement, a glass bowl heaped with tiny and large cherry-red balls set in the center of the country pine table. Faux cheetah fur covers the Louis XIV chairs, a large antique mirror fills one wall, and reproduction Picasso sketches framed in dark wood hang over the fireplace. The sconces are from his shop, and the round sculpture is an Indian ankle bracelet. The mantel is strewn with fresh greens and a garland of brown magnolia leaves. Votive candles and a string of pinecones create an interesting pairing of the grand and the humble.*

LEFT: *The back hallway off the kitchen is a private oasis leading out to a delightful pocket patio for summer enjoyment. The circular stairway leads to Michael's bedroom, giving him access to the house when he has guests sleeping in the front bedrooms. The simple boxwood tree is made in the shop (see page 164 for how you can make one for your home), and the statue of Hercules, an Italian find, sports a wreath made from a leftover sprig of greens. One would expect to find only a white poinsettia in this house.*

mixing simple objects with important pieces, humble with the lofty, this designer has a talent for putting things together that aren't always obvious, such as upholstering Louis XIV chairs with faux cheetah skin and ultrasuede and using them around a country pine table, covering an entire wall in the kitchen with an antique mirror, or painting a gray and ivory checkerboard floor in the hallway. You almost want to say, "Now, why didn't I think of that?"

"When I come home from the shop," he says, "I want a relaxing and calming space." His attitude about decorating is to simplify rather than embellish; during the holidays the serene expanses of white suggest a snowy Christmas. His signature Christmas decoration is a large glass bowl piled with brilliantly shiny red balls, set in the center of the country pine kitchen table.

Michael knows how important flowers are to a room. Fresh flowers welcome guests with fragrance, and he only uses white flowers in his own home. The green stems and leaves provide enough color. The Christmas tree, a few greens, a pinecone garland, candles, and the bright red balls are all that he needs to make the house fit for the holidays.

MAKING A BOXWOOD TREE

Michael Molinar treated us to a demonstration of how to make a boxwood tree at his shop. While he was doing this, his assistant, Jack Bangs, was making one after the other, each with different decorations, for the many holiday parties taking place on the island. "This is a busy time of year," Michael said. "These little boxwood trees make nice table decorations as an alternative to a larger tree or a bouquet of flowers. Anyone can make one of these if they have the material and good tools on hand."

1. *Michael Molinar shows how to make a boxwood tree in his shop, Flowers On Chestnut. He starts with a plastic-lined basket filled with soaking-wet oasis cut to fit. He inserts three sticks through the top to hold the oasis together and secures it with florist's tape so it doesn't move. Tip: Buy the freshest possible product for this project to make it look best and last longer.*

2. *Next, he cuts the sticks flush with the top of the oasis and, starting at the base, pokes the branches of boxwood into the oasis to soften the sharp edges of the container. He advises, "Make the arrangement very full and spilling over as you keep building up and filling in holes. Add small branches wherever you need filler." Tip: If you put the container on a lazy Susan, it will be easy to turn and insert your greens.*

3. *Clip the branches to make them even when needed. He says to keep an eye out for a nice tall, skinny piece to insert in the top. The goal is to make the tree heavier on the bottom, tapering to a point at the top, just like a real tree.*

4. *Dress the miniature tree with a strand of lights and tiny gold and silver balls, pinecones, flowers, or whatever decorations appeal to you. While Michael was making this tree, one covered with fruit, one with gold balls and pinecones and another with roses were being shipped out to various houses around the island. And that was only the first hour of the day!*

On Washing Pond ✦

George Davis's house looks like a forest after a snowfall—everything is white, green, and rustic wood and is an excellent example of how appealingly fresh and versatile a white palette can be. When it is sparingly introduced, such as pink poinsettias in a white urn, color pops out and becomes dramatic rather than expected. This is a house for all seasons but at Christmastime it is especially magical. From every room the owner, an interior designer, has an unobstructed view of Washing Pond, located on one of the island's highest points off Cliff Road. With his signature style of combining an all-white environment with textures of fabrics, warm woods, and discretely selected folk art, architectural remnants, and island accessories, the interior design epitomizes his clean approach so that nothing upstages the scenery. On this day the snow is coming down in heavy flakes, creating a blanket of white at every window and adding to the magical spirit of the season.

Many trips to England have yielded the unusual pieces of furniture and accessories that he freely mixes with decidedly Nantucket pieces. The marine influence is everywhere, from the pond models on the mantel and in his bedroom, to lighthouses and lightship baskets, seashells, and other collectibles from around the island. Some of the pieces are valuable and

ABOVE: *Beads of glass resemble dewdrops resting on the branches, and silver balls reflect the lights, adding overall sparkle. The delicate paper butterfly wings are sprinkled with silver glitter and tiny tree lights glow from within the paper lanterns.*

OPPOSITE: *Every year George Davis designs a Christmas tree with a theme. This year it is Madame Butterfly, and the tabletop tree is covered with Japanese paper lanterns, butterflies, and white paper fans. Whimsy abounds with playful toys and gaily wrapped packages arranged around the bottom of the tree and on chairs. A wooden rocking horse wears a wreath of greens.*

LEFT, TOP: *A bare twig tree is silhouetted in the tall window flanked by two rattan wingback chairs. A glass-top table is covered with collections of shells and scrimshaw, baskets, and small figurines, creating an interesting monochromatic vignette of textures and shapes in keeping with the style of the interior design.*

LEFT, BOTTOM: *Snow is falling on the pond beyond the kitchen window. A large pine tree in the yard is decked out with hundreds of clear Christmas lights, and three frosted-glass snowmen line the windowsill.*

OPPOSITE: *At one end of the living room a built-in scrubbed-pine cabinet is dressed for the holidays with a large evergreen wreath. Unusual wrought-iron reindeer hold votive candles on either side of an urn filled with pink poinsettias. The pine table is from England, where Davis buys most of the furnishings sold through his shop. The painting on the wall, circa 1860–70, is of a French professor at the Sorbonne.*

rare, others are quite ordinary. He likes the freedom and has the confidence to use whatever he likes or finds in his travels or on-island, changing things at whim.

When Davis decorates for Christmas it is done with the same attention to detail and sense of fun and sometimes humor he brings to all his projects. Weeds, his downtown store, on Centre Street, carries the home furnishings and accessories he chooses for the houses he decorates as well as his own homes here and in Key West. His own line of chinaware in a lightship basket pattern, produced by the Wedgwood company, is popular with discerning island homeowners. His designs are minimal and aesthetically charming and reflect his attitude.

Every year George decorates one of the fifty trees for the Festival of Trees. This year his theme was one of his more inventive creations: "A Garden of Eden," complete with a handcrafted shiny emerald snake winding around the tree and intertwined with figures of Adam and Eve. Everyone looks forward to what he'll come up with next year.

The dining room decor is a good example of George Davis's creative and playful nature. A pond model sits on the English cabinet surrounded by greens and nautical touches. The designer then colored little paper boat-signal flags that spell out "Merry Christmas" and attached them to the strings to create a unique decoration in the Nantucket boating tradition.

Simply with Style →×←

Christmas is probably the busiest time of the year for
Kendra Lockley because everyone wants her to cater a
party. Kendra's company, Simply With Style Catering,
is booked solid, sometimes a year in advance, as she has
captured the essence of Nantucket style not only in
what she serves but in how she presents it. Known for
using island ingredients, Kendra and her staff make a
party special. "I do parties for others the way I would do one for myself," she says. "My goal
is to make every little detail perfect, even perhaps more so than the hostess might. I anticipate
what might be needed, like pillows that need replumping when the guests go from cocktails in
to dinner, or restocking the logs in the fireplace so that when they return everything looks
fresh again. My job is to free the hostess up so that, rather than thinking about when to take
the hors d'oeuvres out of the fridge on the day of the party, she can concentrate on choosing
her earrings or the color of the candles." During the holiday season, aside from purely social
events, Kendra caters thank-you parties given by employers at their homes for their
employees. "It's so much more personal than taking them to a restaurant, and everyone
appreciates this show of warmth and giving in a more relaxed environment."

      Once everyone else has been feted, Kendra, her husband, Steve McCluskey, a
former chef and restaurateur, and their young daughter, Merrill, celebrate Christmas with
her extended family, which has been living on Nantucket for a very long time. "My mother

172
→×←
*A Nantucket
Christmas*

ABOVE: *A Christmas doll sits on the long rush-seat bench under the windows in the front hallway.
Kendra made the pinecone garlands when she was a little girl, and she says they are easy to string and
add a simple touch of country decoration to the room. A poinsettia plant is quite elegant in a green urn;
the cast-metal architectural stars over the closet doors look good all year long, but seem especially
appropriate during the holidays.*

OPPOSITE: *Simple green wreaths against the gray shingles welcome visitors at Christmastime to the
home of Kendra Lockley and Steve McCluskey.*

was always active in the Girl Scouts and now this is a very big part of my life," she says. "I grew up making things with my mother and now I do this with my daughter." This includes cookie-making sessions with Merrill, who she wants to be able to one day say, "I did this with my mother when I was a little girl." Right before Christmas Steve, Kendra, and Merrill go out to Moor's End Farm to choose the Christmas tree. "This is a big event for us," she says. "Then we let it sit for a couple of days to relax the branches. When we decorate the tree, we put on a tape of *A Charlie Brown Christmas* and bring out all our handmade ornaments Merrill made from when she was in kindergarten until now."

The Lockley-McCluskey house is located in a family neighborhood on the outskirts of town and is relatively new for an island home. The interior is designed with an open floor plan and is furnished with a decidedly Scandinavian character, combining pine furniture and light colors. It is homey and comfortable, with handmade items, collectibles, and paintings by local artists. Much of the furnishings and folk art come from her sister Liz's shop, the Nantucket Looms. A separate building on the property is where all the cooking and party preparations take place and where Kendra spends most of her time. It is command central. Food plays a big part in the way she decorates for the

A large poinsettia plant in a milk-glass vase, a folk-art doll, mercury-glass balls, and wrapped packages create a delightful Christmas scene on the warm pine cupboard in the living room. Pomegranates heaped in a white ceramic container are the perfect holiday accent on the pine coffee table, and the appliqué snowman pillow adds a playful touch to this pared-down environment.

holidays both in her own home and for the many different tables she arranges for parties. (See page 73 for inspiration.)

The front porch of the home is welcoming in a straightforward, Nantucket way. A simple wreath of greens and another with snowball lights and a bright red bow hang against traditional gray shingles. Inside, one is treated to a decidedly Swedish approach to decorating, with simple garlands made from pinecones strung across each of the windows in the dining alcove. Poinsettias, pomegranates, and tiny crabapples heaped into interesting containers add spots of holiday cheer throughout the rooms. A wonderful pine breakfront holds vintage food tins and a silver bowl filled with an arrangement of winter fruit on the bottom shelf, while the main surface is decorated with a village scene created by Merrill. The kitchen is the family center and is open to the living and dining rooms. Everyone gathers here to participate in the holiday cooking and festivities.

ABOVE: *An unusual wreath is made from white feathers wrapped with red satin ribbon. A few gold and red balls add just the right touch of color.*

OPPOSITE, TOP LEFT: *A country green saltbox holds mail just inside the front door; however, the forgotten mittens, glasses, and hat suggest a recent visit from Santa.*

OPPOSITE, TOP RIGHT: *The red and white patchwork quilt is a Log Cabin pattern resembling a Christmas tree. Kendra often uses the quilt as a table cover for holiday parties.*

OPPOSITE, BOTTOM LEFT: *The pine breakfront holds early food tins, greens from the yard, and a silver bowl filled with an arrangement of winter fruit on the bottom shelf. The top shelf is reserved for Merrill, who is given free rein to create her village scene.*

OPPOSITE, BOTTOM RIGHT: *Kendra found the green jadeite plates from the 1950s years ago at Brimfield, a giant antiques and flea market in Massachusetts. She sets the table with them every Christmas and displays them in the pine plate rack on a narrow wall at the end of the kitchen counter. A green breadbox holding two miniature red chairs and a wire basket heaped with crabapples dotted with sprigs of greens complete this country arrangement.*

KENDRA'S SUGAR COOKIES

In spite of a nonstop schedule, every Christmas mother and daughter bake the eagerly anticipated sugar cookies fancifully decorated and tied into gift packages for Merrill's teachers. "The recipe I use for sugar cookies is a time-honored one that everyone probably has in their collection. It's nothing special but we like it, and we make it special with the cookie cutters we use and the way we decorate them. Anyone can make them and they are always appreciated gifts." Wrapping the cookies in little cellophane bags with raffia or ribbon ties makes them into individual gifts to take to parties, give to teachers, decorate the tree with, or give to guests who come to celebrate the holidays.

2 cups sifted all-purpose flour

¼ tsp. salt

½ tsp. baking powder

1 stick unsalted butter

1 cup sugar

1 large egg

1 tsp. pure vanilla extract

1 tsp. fresh lemon zest

½ tsp. fresh lemon juice

Set oven to 350 degrees F.

Sift together flour, salt, baking powder. Set aside. In a mixer, cream the butter and add sugar. Beat on medium speed for five minutes. Add egg, vanilla, lemon zest, and fresh lemon juice and beat on low, occasionally scraping down the bowl, until thoroughly creamy. Add flour all at once and beat on low until incorporated.

Take dough out of bowl and flatten into a disc. Divide the dough in half for two batches and place in separate plastic bags. Refrigerate for an hour.

Lightly flour dough and roll out to ¼-inch thickness. Cut into cookie shapes and place on an ungreased cookie sheet.

Bake for 8–10 minutes so cookies are light, not browned. Kendra says the decoration is prettier this way.

For icing: Mix together 1 cup of confectioner's sugar, a tablespoonful of lemon juice, and food coloring.

Each batch makes 24–30 cookies.

Every Christmas, Kendra and Merrill bake fanciful sugar cookies to give as gifts. Each cellophane bag is tied with a pretty ribbon and a card for each teacher.

Garlands of pinecones are looped across each of the windows in the sunny dining alcove. Joan Albaugh's landscape oil paintings against the butterscotch walls are perfectly suited to the space. The ivory-colored poinsettia is set in a green bamboo container and flanked by glass candlesticks holding cranberry candles.

In the Holiday Spirit ⇥⤝

When Judy and Bob Seinfeld first saw this house, they knew it was meant for them. Tucked at the end of a private lane off Orange Street, the house is approached through the courtyard. It isn't until you walk around to the back that you notice the breathtaking views of the harbor. The sign over the door says it all, "Karma," and Judy says, "This is a house of love."

Built in the 1820s by a Nantucket sea captain, the house was extensively renovated when the Seinfelds bought it ten years ago. "We saved every single door, hook, and floorboard," Judy says, "in order to retain everything good about the original house." Brent Young, a local builder specializing in early restoration work, is credited with the masterful job of turning it from a wonderful, historic old house into an exquisite home for twenty-first-century living. With the new owners' input it has become comfortable, beautiful, timeless, and chic—a perfect interface of historic character and modern artistry.

One of the unusual features is the stage in the living room. The original owner purchased the house next door, then gutted and annexed it onto this house to create the stage.

ABOVE: *Set high above the harbor, the windows across the back of the living room afford an unobstructed view of Nantucket Bay, where one gets a sense of the comings and goings of seafaring life. Handmade paper star ornaments are artfully arranged in silhouette, seemingly in a random manner, and fill a scallop basket. The lamp base is handmade of aluminum nails.*

OPPOSITE: *A bevy of handmade felt trees creates a winter scene on the piano. Judy says, "I like to celebrate originality and the spirit of creativity." You cannot overdo it with candles for romantic ambience. Filling the top of the piano, lots of votives provide romantic illumination on the stage. The diaphanous curtain, casually draped at the window, adds just the right softness and blends with the snowflakes that billow outdoors.*

When it was first built, local actors would come and perform for visiting friends, and the Seinfelds have carried on this spirited community tradition. Now a player piano is in constant use on the stage and there have been many performances by local drama, poetry, and singing groups. To celebrate the holiday season, neighbors and friends of all ages gather in this lovely setting to hear a trio of singers perform a medley of show tunes. Afterward, small groups gravitate to the piano for an impromptu songfest, as Greta Feeny, our local opera star, offers a gift of "Danny Boy" and happy sounds fill the house. "I like to celebrate the spirit of the season by bringing people together," Judy says.

The house is decorated with all sorts of interesting objects brought back from Bob and Judy's extensive travels and handmade pieces that the couple found special. Asian

OPPOSITE: *Local talent is often showcased on the stage in the Seinfelds' living room. Friends like to gather for a songfest around the player piano as well. The renovation of the house included adding new wide steps in front of the stage to make it more accessible. Simple handmade felt trees cover the top of the piano, and old-fashioned buoys for fishing nets rest under it.*

RIGHT, TOP: *The spirit of the holidays is celebrated here with displays of handcrafted objects such as the sailor's valentine on the table in the living room, the tree-shaped pillow, and stenciled hatboxes filled with giant pinecones.*

RIGHT, BOTTOM: *Simplicity and elegance are demonstrated in the restraint of color in the living room. White tulips clustered in three vases, tall white lilies on the side table, and green leaves punctuate the snowy-white environment. The snowman pillow adds wit and whimsy, and a few scattered pinecones on the table are all that is needed for holiday accents. A boat model by Mark Sutherland and scrimshaw are fine examples of maritime crafts.*

artifacts and maritime collectibles are sprinkled throughout, along with unconventional items from Paris flea markets and auctions on-island. The natural color palette of the interior decor is muted and subtle, and the decorations are restrained and refined, with a little bit of wit and whimsy thrown in for fun. Judy says, "The house provides the perfect environment for all sorts of creativity. I think the holiday season is all about living in peace and celebrating the spirituality that is in all of us. In fact, that is what makes living here so special."

ABOVE, LEFT: *The Tibetan Buddha in the living room is decked out in greens and white roses for a holiday party. Judy's lightship basket usually rests in the statue's folded arms.*

ABOVE, RIGHT: *Warm wood paneling, lots of handcrafts, and paintings by local artists make the small family room a homey place to curl up by the fire. The collection of lightship baskets was made by early Nantucket craftsman Doc Magee and scrimshawed by David Lazarus. Each one has a personal inscription on the bottom. The seaside sketches are by George Harvey, a Cape Cod artist. The papier-mâché and felt Santas come out for the holidays.*

OPPOSITE: *The birthing room from the original house is where Santa's helper hangs his jacket and cap after arriving with Santa by Coast Guard cutter during Christmas Stroll weekend. This was one of Bob's favorite jobs for many years. The collection of blue-and-white Canton ware on the mantel is part of a collection Bob started forty years ago. A folk-art angel sits on a rope chair from the 1940s, part of a set found in Paris.*

A Very Aerie Christmas ⇥⤫⤝

"I love the loftiness of this apartment," says Janis Aldrich, whose spaciously open apartment is conveniently located over her print gallery, and at this time of year when the trees are bare, she has a marvelous view of Nantucket Sound. Janis owns the Janis Aldrich Galleries in Nantucket, New York, and Washington, D.C., where she deals in botanical prints from the seventeenth century to today as well as decorative antique furniture and her signature line of lamps. It is no wonder that the apartment is filled with elegant furnishings and accessories.

Janis had a gallery in town for many years before constructing her own building two years ago. As a woman with impeccable taste who knows exactly what she likes, Janis approaches everything with incredible attention to detail, dedication, and deliberateness. She researched all the past and present architectural styles of Nantucket structures before embarking on her own classic Greek Revival–style building. "I took from the best of the architecture here," she stated. The gallery and her apartment exude comfort with a pedigree. "It isn't a huge space, but I wanted it to be open, with a loftlike feeling," she says. "We used

ABOVE: *An unadorned wreath hangs on the front of the Janis Aldrich Gallery. Lanterns and boxwood trees create symmetry on either side of the imposing doorway of the classic Greek Revival building.*

OPPOSITE: *Janis has no problem with guests overflowing into the bedroom at the other end of the open living room loft, even perched on the bed with a buffet plate in hand. The dark-stained wood floors and molding trim offset the hand-rubbed beadboard walls. Gracefully draped dark green velvet panels puddle to the floor on each side of the windows hung with simple beaded wreaths. An ivory brocade bedspread, a velvet bed skirt, an angel on the night table, and a few greens in a magazine holder create an inviting place for a sip of champagne. With disarming spontaneity, Janis adds a last-minute touch by simply tying the draperies back with a strand of beads.*

all the space quite efficiently, and a lot of the interest comes from the high ceilings, different angles, and exposed heating ducts. It's so unusual for Nantucket, and I love having this apartment over the gallery," she says. A deep, generous sofa, large coffee table, and chairs of ample size focus on the loftlike quality of the room. Pull-up chairs offer the flexibility to create intimacy within the large, open space.

Janis often hosts brunches here to preview an artist's work, and friends of the gallery enjoy the relaxed and homey atmosphere she creates. This Christmas Janis has invited several guests to meet a new decorative artist she is introducing, Jonas Everets of New York City.

As with her many endeavors, Janis never does the expected, and decorating for the holidays is no different. She sticks with her beautifully subtle palette of ethereal, rich colors like those used throughout the apartment and absolutely rejects any hint of Christmas green or red. The Christmas tree is encircled with yards of apricot-colored organdy ribbon and covered with dozens of fuchsia and purple ornaments and hundreds of lights. Packages under the tree are wrapped in handmade Japanese rice paper in colors such as persimmon, aubergine, eggplant, celadon, and gold and lavishly tied up in ribbons of medieval colors. Elaborate bows embellish each one as the final touch of flattery.

OPPOSITE: *A stairway from the gallery leads up to the loft apartment on the second floor. The fireplace ledge in the living room is carefully decorated with a cache of treasures. Bunches of clear-glass beaded grapes hang from the greens dotted with beeswax candles in alabaster holders. Star ornaments and silver swans provide different shapes and textures. Old English wall sconces are embellished with reverse painting on glass.*

ABOVE: *Four-foot-tall green Merino glass vases are grouped together on the landing for a dramatic still-life arrangement against the green and gold wallpaper. Never settling for the expected, Janis shuns what might seem like an obvious choice in favor of lavish, plump pink peonies and sterling roses fresh from Trillium (see page 74). The print on the wall is from the gallery.*

OVERLEAF: *The Christmas tree fills one corner of the loftlike living room. An evergreen and pinecone wreath hangs in one window, while the curves of the side windows are accentuated with ropes of beaded grapes. Frosted fruit and clusters of candles brighten the glass-topped coffee table. The dining-turned-wrapping table is covered with layers of plum-colored, hand-dyed natural linen. Throughout the apartment Janis has elevated natural materials with measured doses of silks, brocades, tapestry, embroidery, cashmere, and velvet. A handcrafted, shell-covered terra-cotta pot holds pine branches mixed with artificial stems of beaded glass that shimmer like icy dewdrops in the candlelight.*

Acknowledgments ➝✂︎←

It was Thursday at the beginning of the Nantucket Stroll weekend and the island was abuzz with activity—town workers were stringing lights on the Christmas trees for the ceremonial lighting of the trees that would take place the next evening at sundown. Store owners were hanging wreaths on doorways and filling their window boxes with seasonal greens and twigs of berries. A volunteer group was decorating the monument at the foot of Main Street, and suddenly it began to snow—big, beautiful flakes, the kind that stick, came down as if on cue. Within minutes the cobblestones were covered with a dusting of white. Schoolchildren in colorful parkas were having a snowball fight in the library park. Squeals of laughter permeated the air. Nantucket was becoming a magical winter wonderland in time for the biggest weekend of the season. How lucky could we get?—a Christmas book with a snowy background. It was a photographer's dream. And that's just the way this entire project went from beginning to end, like a dream.

Nantucket is my home and I have had a love affair with the island for more than thirty years. Living here brings people closer. There is a shared sense of pride in the island and an awareness that it is a privilege to live here. It was therefore with extreme joy and appreciation that I approached this project. Christmastime on this island is right out of a fairy tale, but it is a very brief time—decorating, entertaining, visiting, making merry, and reveling in the seasonal changes is compressed into three weeks.

Designed by architect Frederick Brown Coleman, the Nantucket Atheneum Library was completed after the original building was completely destroyed in the Great Fire of 1846. Many great luminaries lectured here, including Ralph Waldo Emerson, Henry David Thoreau, Horace Greeley, Lucretia Mott, Frederick Douglass, and Maria Mitchell. The 1996 renovation and restoration reopened the second-floor Great Hall for lectures and research, provided gallery and conference space on the lower level, and created the Weezie Library for Children. The library currently maintains a forty-thousand-volume collection. A simple wreath adorns the front door, and when it snows, the happy sounds of children having a snowball fight can be heard in the library park adjacent to the building.

When we first sat down with the staff at Bulfinch Press in the Time & Life Building it was with apprehension. Could a project of this magnitude possibly be finished in just one Christmas season? The answer was simply no. It would take two years, and this meant a lot of planning and contacting people who would be willing to commit their homes to the project. More important, we were asking them to decorate as they would normally, only well ahead of December 25.

Over the years I have been in hundreds of Nantucket homes, and there are more wonderful houses in this small area than we could possibly include. But even more remarkable are the people who own these houses. Collectively they represent an extraordinary sense of style and sensitivity to the island and the houses in which they live. The hardest part about doing this book was choosing the houses. It was our goal to include a wide variety of architectural and decorating styles: some historic, some new, delightful little cottages and grand houses from Nantucket's prosperous whaling days, as well as artists' homes and the houses of the designers, florists, and caterers who contribute to these beautiful interiors and the holiday parties showcased here.

I first want to thank everyone at Bulfinch Press for originating this project. It would not have happened without the encouragement and support of publisher Jill Cohen and associate publisher Karen Murgolo. Their enthusiasm and insight proved to be well founded. Once more I'm incredibly grateful for the most perfect editor, Karyn Gerhard, who, in her words, "is totally into Christmas." No one could be more understanding, professional, and sensitive to an author's plight or the subject. Thanks also to Margaret Pai and Matthew Ballast for everything they do on behalf of my books at Bulfinch, and to Joel Averon's team for their wonderfully fresh approach to design. A special thank-you to my agent, Linda Konner, who is encouraging and always watching out for my best interests. Without her insight for teaming me up with a wonderful group of publishing experts, I would not have had this most rewarding of projects.

Most important, I want to thank my husband and partner, Jon Aron, for helping with the art direction of the photography and organizing the material for the book. I rely on his experience for the success of any project we produce together. Working on this book was a joy because of Jeff Allen. His wide range of experience is what he brought to this project, and the results are incredibly intuitive, sensitive photographs. Jon and I worked on this project with Jeff over a two-year period, and in that time, no matter what we asked him to shoot, he always had the same cheerful answer: "No problem." This is what working with Jeff is all about.

But it is to the people who contributed to this book that I owe the most gratitude, for it was their gracious hospitality and willingness to go all out in decorating their homes that ultimately made this book exciting. I am also deeply appreciative to all the people in town who gave of their talents and shared their expertise as well. Thank you all for your time and effort, incredibly good taste, and willingness to share with us your approach to the holidays: Joan Albaugh, Janis Aldrich, Robin Bergland and her staff, the staff at The Brotherhood, Elizabeth Brown, Roy and Kathy Clauss, Jim and Mellie Cooper, George Davis, Debbie Deeley, Donna Elle of Donna Elle Interior Design, Antje Farber, Ernie and Kay Frank, Jenny Garneau, Toby Greenberg, Peggy and Eli Kaufman, Glenora Kelly-Smith, Richard Kemble and George Korn, Thomas Koon and Bart Cosgrove, All and Andrea Kovalencik, Judy Lee and Robert Schwartzenbach, Kendra Lockley and her staff, Holly McGowan of Coastal Design, Ian and Carolyn MacKenzie, Michael Molinar, Jackie Peterson, Dorothy Slover and Doug Kenwood, Judy and Bob Seinfeld, Luraye Tate, Kathleen Walsh and Brent Young, John West, Margaret Mary Wilkes, and Jeff's assistant Maureen Riley for being a real sport and always knowing just where I left my glasses.

—Leslie Linsley

Email: leslie@leslielinsley.com